TOBACCO

BY CAROL HAND

CONTENT CONSULTANT

BRANDON HENDERSON, PHD

ASSISTANT PROFESSOR, DEPARTMENT OF BIOMEDICAL SCIENCES
JOAN C. EDWARDS SCHOOL OF MEDICINE AT MARSHALL UNIVERSITY

Essential Library

An Imprint of Abdo Publishing | abdopublishing.com

Published by Abdo Publishing, a division of ABDO, PO Box 398166, Minneapolis, Minnesota 55439.
Copyright © 2019 by Abdo Consulting Group, Inc. International copyrights reserved in all countries.
No part of this book may be reproduced in any form without written permission from the publisher.
Essential Library™ is a trademark and logo of Abdo Publishing.

Printed in the United States of America, North Mankato, Minnesota
022018
092018

**THIS BOOK CONTAINS
RECYCLED MATERIALS**

Cover Photo: Gitte Moller/iStockphoto
Interior Photos: C. Stewart/iStockphoto, 4–5; AFP/Getty Images, 8; Phil Pell/iStockphoto, 12;
Shutterstock Images, 15, 26–27, 52–53; Antonia Gros/Shutterstock Images, 18–19; Red Line Editorial,
20, 36, 88–89; iStockphoto, 23, 63, 91; Mukhtar Khan/AP Images, 24; Hulton Archive/Getty Images,
29; HWG/AP Images, 32; Jamie Gill/AP Images, 35; Pablo Martinez Monsivais/AP Images, 38–39; Khin
Maung Win/AP Images, 41; Scott Camazine/Science Source, 43; Arthur Glauberman/Science Source,
46; Phanie/Science Source, 48–49; Eye of Science/Science Source, 56; SPL/Science Source, 61, 75;
People Images/iStockphoto, 68; Faye Norman/Science Source, 70–71; Steve Helber/AP Images,
79; Daniel Bockwoldt/picture-alliance/dpa/AP Images, 84; Mitsuru Tamura/Yomiuri Shimbun/AP
Images, 86–87; Wilson Ring/AP Images, 95; Doug Martin/Science Source, 98

Editor: Arnold Ringstad
Series Designer: Laura Polzin

Library of Congress Control Number: 2017961357

Publisher's Cataloging-in-Publication Data

Names: Hand, Carol, author.
Title: Tobacco / by Carol Hand.
Description: Minneapolis, Minnesota : Abdo Publishing, 2019. | Series: Drugs in real life | Includes
      online resources and index.
Identifiers: ISBN 9781532114212 (lib.bdg.) | ISBN 9781532154041 (ebook)
Subjects: LCSH: Tobacco products--Juvenile literature. | Nicotine addiction--Juvenile literature.
      | Tobacco use--Health aspects--Juvenile literature. | Drug control--United States--
      Juvenile literature.
Classification: DDC 362.296--dc23

CONTENTS

TOBACCO OR NO TOBACCO?

Kindra Tanner started smoking at age 13. She smoked her first cigarette because she was angry with her mother, who had forbidden her from seeing a boy she liked. A friend offered her a cigarette, and after smoking it, she immediately felt better. At first, Kindra says, "You feel good—refreshed, like drinking water after running all day."[1] She continued smoking.

Kindra is typical of teens who start smoking, says Jonathan Klein, a pediatrician at the University of Rochester. They are led by friends, movies, television, and advertising to see smoking as a way to relax and to cope with problems. Kindra's mother noticed the smell of smoke on Kindra's clothes, but she just thought she

Nearly all smokers began using tobacco as teenagers.

was hanging out with other kids who smoked. Then, Kindra was caught smoking at school and was suspended. With her mother's help, she finally quit, but it took months. Starting was much easier than stopping.

STUDENT OPINIONS

Three-fourths of adults surveyed favor the Tobacco 21 Initiative. But how do kids and teens feel about it? In 2017, a professor at Children's Mercy Hospital in Kansas City, Missouri, asked more than 17,000 youths aged 11 to 18. Of students who did not smoke cigarettes or e-cigarettes, 71 percent supported raising the age for tobacco purchases. But only 17 percent of young cigarette smokers and 31 percent of e-cigarette smokers supported the measure.[3]

TOBACCO 21 INITIATIVE

Because their brains are still undergoing significant changes, teens are more likely to become smokers than adults. The nicotine in tobacco products changes their brain development, and they often become addicted. To counter teen smoking, the Preventing Tobacco Addiction Foundation is sponsoring the Tobacco 21 Initiative, which seeks to raise the minimum age for buying tobacco products from 18 to 21. The foundation is targeting teens such as Kindra, and its reasons are based on evidence. Smokers almost always begin experimenting with tobacco products as teens or preteens.

The Preventing Tobacco Addiction Foundation believes prohibiting tobacco use in teens and preteens will lower tobacco-related risks, including addiction. In addition to the Tobacco 21 Initiative, it supports increasing tobacco education in schools, less media exposure for tobacco products, more advertising on the dangers of smoking, and more tobacco-free areas in homes, schools, and public places. The Tobacco 21 Initiative is gaining momentum across the country. By August 2017, more than 250 US cities and counties and three states—California, Hawaii, and New Jersey—had raised the age for purchasing tobacco to 21.[4]

WORLD NO TOBACCO DAY

Smoking is a worldwide concern. The World Health Organization (WHO), part of the United Nations (UN), created World No Tobacco Day in 1987. It is commemorated every year on May 31. This initiative calls

POTENTIAL RESULTS OF ADOPTING TOBACCO 21

A national survey in 2010 found that approximately 95 percent of adults with nicotine addictions had started smoking before age 21.[5] If the Tobacco 21 policy is adopted throughout the United States, one study estimated that people born between 2010 and 2019 would have 249,000 fewer premature deaths and 45,000 fewer lung cancer deaths.[6] A March 2015 study by the Institute of Medicine predicted that 25 percent fewer youths would start smoking, overall smoking rates would decline 12 percent, and there would be 16,000 fewer preterm and low-birth-weight babies per year.[7]

on governments around the world to control tobacco use. It recommends banning tobacco advertising, requiring public places to be smoke free, and advocating plain packaging and higher taxes for tobacco products. Why does WHO care whether people smoke?

WHO, and people around the world, care about smoking because smoking kills. Every year, more than seven million people die from smoking-related causes. Smoking also has monetary costs. Every year, families and governments spend more than $1.4 trillion for health-care costs and lost productivity due to tobacco use. On World No Tobacco Day in 2017, WHO director-general Dr. Margaret Chan stated, "Tobacco threatens us

Bangladeshi anti-smoking activists celebrated World No Tobacco Day in 1999 by burning packs of cigarettes.

all. Tobacco [worsens] poverty, reduces economic productivity, contributes to poor household food choices, and pollutes indoor air."[8]

The United Nations and its member states are committed to the UN's 2030 Agenda for Sustainable Development. This agenda includes a one-third reduction in premature deaths from noncommunicable diseases (NCDs) by the year 2030. NCDs include circulatory and respiratory diseases, cancer, and diabetes. Tobacco use is a major risk factor for all of these diseases. Meeting the goal will therefore involve following the 2005 WHO Framework Convention on Tobacco Control. This is the first global public health treaty, and it affirms that all people should have the highest health standards. It is based on scientific evidence of the devastating effects of tobacco use on human health, society, economies, and the environment.

SAVING LIVES AND DOLLARS

In January 2017, the World Health Organization and the US National Cancer Institute published a major report on tobacco use and control. The report stated that, worldwide, there are 1.1 billion tobacco smokers 15 and older. Eighty percent of smokers live in low- or middle-income countries, many in poverty. If all countries raised cigarette taxes by $0.80 per pack, the report predicted that smoking rates would decline by 9 percent and that there would be 66 million fewer adult smokers.[9]

THE TOBACCO INDUSTRY FIGHTS BACK

Not everyone is on board with cutting tobacco use. According to Dr. Vinayak Prasad, director of WHO's tobacco control project, "The [tobacco] industry tends to interfere in the policy-making process. So there are intimidating practices, they threaten, they use myths about the contribution to the economy."[10] WHO says tobacco companies use lawsuits to block progress on tobacco regulation policies. Even unsuccessful lawsuits may slow progress for years. In May 2017, after a legal battle that lasted five years, the World Trade Organization (WTO) upheld an Australian law restricting tobacco packaging.

In the United States, a 1998 lawsuit brought by 46 states against the four largest US tobacco companies resulted in the Master Tobacco Settlement Agreement. The companies agreed not to target minors in their advertising, but critics have pointed out that they are not living up to this promise. In 2006, US District Court judge Gladys Kessler said, "Defendants

SOME GROUPS DEFEND SMOKING

The Smokers Association is a group founded to defend people "who expect from life the freedom to smoke, drink, eat and to enjoy personal lifestyle choices without restrictions or interferences."[11] Members of this group feel that governments should not infringe on any lifestyle or cultural choices, including smoking. Some feel that scientific evidence for the dangers of smoking is weak or misrepresented by scientists. One member, Patrick Basham, thinks tobacco policy is based on unscientific claims from research done by anti-tobacco groups.

continue to engage in many practices which target youth, and deny that they do so."[12] In 2014, the US surgeon general said, "The tobacco industry aggressively markets and promotes lethal and addictive products, and continues to recruit youths and young adults as new consumers of these products."[13] In response, the tobacco industry argues that rather than targeting youths, its companies' advertising budgets are only being used to stay competitive with other tobacco companies.

IS THERE A RIGHT TO SMOKE?

The tug-of-war between the tobacco industry and those trying to control smoking has advocates on both sides. But the law is on the side of

DOES THE CONSTITUTION PROTECT SMOKERS?

The Due Process Clause of the US Constitution states that the government cannot deprive individuals of a right without "due process of law." That is, the government must have a reasonable justification for removing the right. A higher standard is set for the few rights specifically guaranteed by the Constitution. Right-to-smoke groups often cite one of these, the right to privacy. However, the US Supreme Court has ruled that while this right protects individuals' decisions about reproduction and family relationships, it does not protect smoking.

Right-to-smoke advocates also point to the Equal Protection Clause. This part of the Constitution states that all groups of people are entitled to "equal protection of the laws." Smoking advocates contend that this clause should protect smokers as a group. Courts disagree. In most cases, the government must prove only that its discrimination against smokers is rational and related to a "legitimate goal," such as maintaining a healthy workplace.[14]

smoking regulation. In public spaces, including workplaces, the right to smoke is increasingly counterbalanced by the right of nonsmokers to breathe clean, smoke-free air. Nonsmokers became more vocal as evidence of the health effects of smoking

Bans on indoor smoking have become common in the United States in recent decades.

began to pile up in the 1960s. Nonsmoker Thomas Greenwood stated his case in a 1988 letter to the New York Times: "No one has the right to impair the health of a fellow employee; everyone has the right to breathe clean air."[15]

In 2015, approximately 15.1 percent of US adults 18 and over were smokers. This was down from 20.9 percent in 2005.[16] Younger people are smoking less, too. According to the Centers for Disease Control and Prevention (CDC), in 2016, 20 percent of high school students used at least one tobacco product in the 30 days before the survey. About 11.3 percent had used e-cigarettes, down from 16 percent the year before. About 8 percent smoked traditional cigarettes, and 7.7 percent smoked cigars.[17]

While many youths still smoke, Matthew Myers, president of the Campaign for Tobacco-Free Kids, is encouraged. He points out that teenage cigarette smoking has dropped drastically in recent years. But, he cautions, hard work is necessary to ensure a continuing downward trend in tobacco use.

"The dramatic, long-term decline in youth cigarette smoking is a public health success story of extraordinary importance."[18]

—Matthew Myers, president of the Campaign for Tobacco-Free Kids

CHAPTER TWO

WHAT IS TOBACCO?

Tobacco is one of the world's most important agricultural plants. Although native to North America, it can grow in any warm, moist environment. It is cultivated on all continents except Antarctica. China is the world's largest tobacco grower, followed by Brazil and India. The United States is fourth. In 2016, the United States grew 629 million pounds (285 million kg) of tobacco, with a value of $1.27 billion.[1] Most of the world's tobacco is made into cigarettes.

Tobacco is grown in more than 120 nations.

TOBACCO: ITS DANGEROUS CHEMICALS

According to the American Lung Association, cigarettes contain more than 600 ingredients.[2] In addition to the tobacco itself, they contain filters, paper, and hundreds of additives that add flavoring, make the smoke easier to inhale, and enhance the addictiveness of the cigarette. During smoking, cigarettes release more than 7,000 chemicals, at least 69 of which are carcinogenic, or cancer causing.[3] Cigarettes, cigars, and pipe tobacco are all made from dried tobacco leaves. Many other ingredients are added to improve taste and make smoking more pleasant. The chemicals produced during smoking result from burning tobacco and its additives. Chemicals found in tobacco smoke include nicotine, hydrogen cyanide, lead, arsenic, formaldehyde, ammonia, benzene, carbon monoxide, nitrosamines, and polycyclic aromatic hydrocarbons (PAHs).

"When the chemicals in cigarettes are inhaled, they put our bodies into a state of physical stress by sending literally thousands of poisons, toxic metals and carcinogens coursing through our bloodstream with every puff we take."[4]

—Smoking cessation advocate
Terry Martin

Many chemicals in tobacco smoke are dangerous. The carcinogen benzene is found in pesticides and gasoline, but half of all human exposure to benzene comes from cigarette smoke. Formaldehyde, which is used to embalm dead bodies, and vinyl chloride, which is used in plastics and cigarette filters, are carcinogens. Arsenic and cadmium are toxic heavy metals. Arsenic is a component of many poisons, including pesticides used on tobacco fields. Cadmium is found in batteries. Lead-210 and polonium-210 are toxic, radioactive heavy metals. Other highly poisonous chemicals in tobacco smoke include ammonia, carbon monoxide, and hydrogen cyanide.

Nearly 500 of the dangerous chemicals in tobacco smoke are polycyclic aromatic hydrocarbons (PAHs). These organic chemicals are similar in structure to benzene. They are both carcinogenic and mutagenic, causing increased mutations in DNA. PAHs are formed when tobacco and its additives are incompletely burned during smoking.

Cigarette tar is the sticky yellowish-brown substance left behind when cigarettes are burned. It consists of a combination of organic and inorganic chemicals, including carbon dioxide, carbon monoxide, and volatile organic compounds. Breathing tar paralyzes and eventually degrades the cilia, the tiny hairs that line and protect the nose and throat.

RADIOACTIVITY AND CIGARETTES

Lead-210 and polonium-210 are radioactive particles present in cigarette smoke. Both come from uranium, a chemical element present in nature in small amounts. Uranium breaks down to release another element, radium. Radium in soil then decays into radon gas. This process frees tiny radioactive particles of lead and polonium. These attach to fine hairs on the undersurfaces of tobacco leaves and end up in cigarettes. During smoking, they are breathed in and collect in smokers' lungs.

Nicotine naturally occurs in the crushed tobacco leaves that are smoked in cigarettes.

This allows tar to enter the lungs, where it collects. Tar is a major cause of lung and throat cancer in smokers. It also causes yellow-brown stains on teeth and fingers.

Cigar smoke contains approximately the same chemicals found in cigarette smoke, but in different proportions. Cigar tobacco is aged and fermented, causing it to produce large amounts of nitrates and nitrites. When burned, these substances produce nitrosamines, which are extremely potent carcinogens.

Also, cigars burn less completely than cigarettes. This results in higher concentrations of harmful substances, including nitrogen oxides, ammonia, carbon monoxide, and tar.

TOBACCO: ITS ADDICTIVE POTENTIAL

The chemical most often associated with smoking is tobacco's addictive component, nicotine. Addiction to nicotine is the second-leading cause of death in the world. It is the leading cause of preventable death. In the United States, cigarette smoking causes more than 480,000 deaths per year, or more than 1,300 per day.[5] Nicotine is toxic, and it can severely damage health. Due to nicotine and other chemicals, smoking tobacco is a major risk factor in circulatory disease.

Every time a smoker takes a "hit" on a cigarette, nicotine enters the bloodstream. It causes a reaction within seconds. The body secretes adrenaline, which increases blood pressure, heart rate, and respiration. Nicotine also increases release of the brain chemical dopamine, which causes feelings of pleasure and energy. However, these feelings fade rapidly. Once a person's

This partial list of the compounds found in cigarette smoke demonstrates how each component can have multiple effects on the body.

WHAT'S IN CIGARETTE SMOKE?

	Carcinogen	Toxic to Lungs	Toxic to Heart and Blood Vessels	Toxic to Reproductive Systems and Development	Addictive
Acetaldehyde	X	X			X
Acetone		X			
Ammonia		X			
Arsenic	X		X	X	
Benzene	X		X	X	
Cadmium	X	X		X	
Carbon monoxide				X	
Ethylene oxide	X	X		X	
Lead	X		X	X	
Mercury	X			X	
Nicotine				X	X
Nitrobenzene	X	X		X	
Phenol		X	X		
Toluene		X		X	
Vinyl acetate	X	X			

body is used to receiving nicotine, he or she begins to suffer withdrawal symptoms, such as irritability, anxiety, sweating, and intestinal problems, when nicotine is taken away. These symptoms can only be relieved by smoking again. The body quickly builds up a tolerance to nicotine, so the person must smoke more and more to maintain the positive sensations.

Cigarettes are particularly addictive because they get nicotine into the brain so quickly. Tobacco users who do not usually inhale the smoke, such as pipe smokers, cigar smokers, or smokeless tobacco users, absorb nicotine through the mucous membranes of the mouth and throat. Here, nicotine reaches peak levels in the blood and brain more slowly. However nicotine is delivered, children and teens appear to be especially sensitive to it, and they are more likely to become addicted. Research suggests that three of every four people who begin smoking in high school will smoke as adults.[6]

Behavioral changes signal addiction to nicotine. The person smokes more over time and is unable to quit. The person craves tobacco and goes to great lengths to get it. This need may cause problems with relationships or prevent the person from fulfilling obligations for work, school, or family. Those addicted to nicotine may pay high prices for it, even if they cannot afford basic needs. The addiction may lead to dangerous behaviors, such as smoking in bed or continued smoking despite harmful health effects. People may even keep smoking after major throat surgeries done to treat their smoking-related problems. And they undergo withdrawal if tobacco use stops.

TOBACCO: ITS DELIVERY ROUTES

Most people take in tobacco by smoking or burning it. Chewing tobacco without burning it is rising in popularity. A third method of nicotine delivery is expanding rapidly: Electronic Nicotine Delivery Systems (ENDS).

Smoking products include cigarettes, cigars, bidis, kreteks, pipes, and hookahs. Tobacco for cigarettes goes through a curing process and is then finely cut, combined with many additives, and rolled into a paper cylinder, often with a filter on one end. Cigarettes imported into the United States include bidis from Southeast Asia and kreteks from Indonesia. Bidis may be flavored with chocolate or cherry. Kreteks are flavored with cloves. Both deliver more nicotine, carbon monoxide, and tar than conventional cigarettes. They are more addictive and cause more serious disease than conventional cigarettes.

Cigars, cigarillos, and little cigars are made of air-cured tobacco that is aged, fermented, and wrapped in tobacco leaves. Fermentation changes the taste and odor of the tobacco. Cigars have more nicotine than cigarettes. Little cigars and cigarillos are smaller and often flavored.

Pipes are used to smoke loose tobacco. The tobacco is lit in a bowl, and the smoke is drawn and inhaled through a stem and

Breathing tobacco smoke quickly delivers its toxic chemicals to the bloodstream.

mouthpiece. In a hookah, the tobacco is heated using charcoal and then drawn through water. The water is meant to remove impurities, but hookah smoke still contains many toxins. During a hookah session, the smoker takes in 100 to 200 times the amount of smoke obtained from a single cigarette.[7]

Chewed, or smokeless, tobacco includes chewing tobacco and snuff. Chewing tobacco may be in loose-leaf form, made into strips. It may also come in two other forms: pieces known as soft or hard plugs. Chewing tobacco is crushed with the teeth to release its nicotine. Snuff is moist and finely chopped. It is not chewed, but placed between the cheek and gum. In both cases, nicotine is absorbed through the mucous membranes of the mouth, and the tobacco juice is spit out.

The hookah is a popular smoking device in India and nearby countries.

Electronic cigarettes (e-cigarettes), vaporizers, vape pens, hookah pens, and e-pipes are all names for ENDS. ENDS use a liquid that contains nicotine, flavorings, and various additives, some toxic and carcinogenic. The liquid is heated to form a vapor that the user inhales. ENDS may resemble cigarettes, cigars, pipes, or a variety of other shapes. Some are slightly larger, with small tanks to hold the liquid. E-cigarettes are battery powered and usually have replaceable cartridges. They do not contain tobacco, so they produce no smoke. But, because they contain nicotine and other toxins, they are still addictive and disease causing.

People take in nicotine in many ways. Some choose alternatives to cigarettes because

THE RISE OF E-CIGARETTES

E-cigarettes were introduced to the United States in 2007. So far, regulatory agencies are not convinced they are safe. The Food and Drug Administration (FDA) has shown that not all ingredients are disclosed and that nicotine levels do not always match the amount listed on the labels. In 2014, the FDA proposed regulations for e-cigarettes, including disclosing all ingredients and not selling them to minors. Manufacturers object to FDA regulation because they consider e-cigarettes recreational products rather than drugs. E-cigarettes are rapidly rising in popularity. Many smokers consider them to be less dangerous than cigarettes and think they can quit smoking by switching to e-cigarettes, which are tobacco-free. An e-cigarette habit is usually cheaper than smoking tobacco cigarettes, and using these products is allowed in some areas that prohibit smoking.

"There is no safe level of tobacco use."[8]

—National Cancer Institute

The precise health effects of e-cigarettes are still under study, but it is clear that nicotine is a harmful chemical regardless of how it is taken into the body.

they believe they can get the pleasures of nicotine without the

health problems associated with smoking. But studies show

that, no matter what method is used, the body receives large

concentrations of nicotine and other toxic chemicals. This means there is no safe concentration of nicotine and no safe way to take in tobacco.

TOBACCO IN AMERICA

Smoking tobacco has long been a religious experience for many indigenous people of the Americas. Later, it became a major industry throughout Europe and the Americas, as well as a common social ritual. Only since the 1960s has smoking been discouraged and even regulated. How did these changes in attitudes toward tobacco come to pass?

HISTORY OF SMOKING

Around 1000 BCE, the Maya began to smoke and chew the plant. They also mixed it with other herbs and used it to treat wounds. As the Maya migrated to other parts of North and South America,

Tobacco became a valuable crop to the European colonists, particularly when they turned to slavery for their labor force

they took tobacco with them. Tobacco was also important to Native Americans in North America. Some tribes' oral histories include stories of how creators gave tobacco to the tribes' ancestors. The plant was smoked in sacred ceremonies.

Christopher Columbus observed Native people smoking in Cuba. Jean Nicot, the French ambassador to Portugal, first took tobacco to England and France in 1560. He became rich selling it to Europeans. The genus name of tobacco, *Nicotiana*, is derived from Nicot. So is the name of its addictive active ingredient: nicotine. By 1600, tobacco use in Europe was widespread, and by 1700, Europe had a full-fledged tobacco industry. In North America, tobacco planters forced enslaved people to work on their plantations, boosting their profits and creating a major industry. By the mid-1700s, the tobacco industry was the largest user of slave labor in the United States.

Even in the early days, physicians recognized tobacco's health risks. In 1602, an anonymous author compared the illnesses of chimney sweeps with those of smokers. In 1795, German doctor Samuel Thomas von Sömmerring observed lip cancers in pipe smokers. American physician Benjamin Rush wrote about the dangers of tobacco in 1798. By the 1920s, doctors began to link smoking with lung cancer. In the 1950s and 1960s, several major reports implicated tobacco use in a variety of serious illnesses.

By that time, the tobacco industry was a major force in both Europe and the United States. Advertising increased sales, and tobacco companies influenced political parties. During both world wars, the US military gave its soldiers free cigarettes to boost morale. Smoking was

first regulated in the United States in 1964, when a historic US surgeon general's report definitively linked smoking to lung cancer. This led to health warnings on cigarette packages and bans on radio and television advertising of tobacco. Restrictions on smoking in US public places began in 1973. In 1988, the surgeon general concluded that research definitively proved that nicotine was addictive. The tobacco industry fought back, launching marketing and public relations campaigns that sought to distort the scientific research on the dangers of smoking. As research on the dangers of tobacco accumulated, tobacco companies had less influence. People began to sue them for damages to their own health or for the deaths of relatives.

WHY PEOPLE SMOKE

"However bad you thought smoking was, it's even worse."[2]

—*Journalist Denise Grady, New York Times, 2015*

There is seldom a single reason why any individual starts smoking. Young people may take it up if their parents are smokers. Teens and preteens are twice as likely to smoke if one or both parents smoke. Teens are also strongly influenced by peer pressure. They often feel a mixture of independence and insecurity. If peers keep offering

them cigarettes, they may accept to fit in. Teens also engage in

risk-taking behavior, or the thrill of breaking rules. Cigarettes are

US surgeon general Luther Terry presented the bombshell 1964 report that detailed the health effects of smoking.

readily available, and smoking is an easy way to rebel. Young people may think smoking makes them look more mature because they are doing something adults do. Finally, teens are at an increased risk of taking up smoking if they have suffered from traumatic events.

Advertising strongly affects the tendency to smoke. One of the earliest techniques for decreasing smoking was to regulate or ban advertising. In 1970, President Richard Nixon signed legislation that banned tobacco advertising on television and on the radio. Ads still appeared elsewhere, including in magazines. In the United States during the 1990s, internal emails from tobacco companies showed that these companies were targeting advertising at young people to attract new smokers. Courts ruled that the companies were responsible for the effects of their products. A portion of the money that once targeted

TOBACCO MISINFORMATION

Smokers hear considerable misinformation about smoking. In the United States, past tobacco ads still linger in the public consciousness. For example, the iconic Marlboro man, often a cowboy, portrays smoking as masculine. Some cigarette ads even showed doctors endorsing particular brands. In Japan, some cigarette advertising claims smoking increases health and vitality. More common in the United States are myths that light cigarettes are less dangerous than regular cigarettes, or that the danger varies by brand. People who believe this misinformation may switch brands or switch to light cigarettes, thinking they are making a healthier choice, rather than quit.

new smokers was diverted to campaigns promoting health care and smoking cessation. Media products, such as movies and television, can also encourage smoking. When people see a character they admire smoking, they tend to view smoking as desirable and socially acceptable.

TEEN TOBACCO USE

Tobacco use among American teenagers is declining, but it is still high. In 2016, 7.2 percent of middle school students and 20 percent of high school students used some type of tobacco product. Seventeen percent of high school girls and 23.5 percent of high school boys used tobacco. Cigarette use is declining, but e-cigarette use is growing. Young smokers, who often used flavored cigarettes, have moved to e-cigarettes following legal restrictions on normal cigarette flavoring enacted in 2009. If smoking continues at its current rate, about 5.6 million Americans who were under age 18 in 2016 will later die of tobacco-related illnesses.[3]

There are many factors and reasons behind the popularity of smoking. Poor and less-educated people are more likely to smoke. Some people have a genetic tendency toward addiction. Smokers may start—or continue—smoking for the feelings it gives them. Some use it for self-medication because they feel better when they smoke. Depressed or anxious people show decreased symptoms when they smoke. Some feel decreased appetite, and they use smoking to lose weight. Others use smoking to mask poor social skills or low self-esteem. Perhaps most

TEEN USE OF
CIGARETTES VS. E-CIGARETTES
IN THE PAST MONTH, BASED ON A 2015 SURVEY

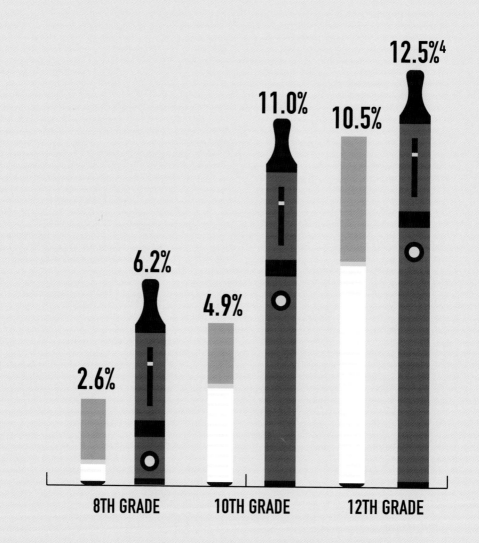

2.6%

6.2%

4.9%

11.0%

10.5%

12.5%[4]

8TH GRADE   10TH GRADE   12TH GRADE

often, people smoke to reduce the stress of work, school, or other life situations. But all of these reasons eventually backfire. Smoking and other forms of tobacco use all come with a host of dangerous side effects. They can quickly become a chemical and psychological crutch.

SMOKING TODAY

A 2015 study on the hazards of tobacco followed the smoking habits of almost one million people for ten years. Previously, tobacco was known to cause 500,000 US deaths per year. The new study showed that it caused 60,000 more than this. Before the study, tobacco was known to cause 21 diseases, including 12 types of cancer.[5] The study added more: increased risk of infection, kidney disease, intestinal disease due to inadequate blood flow, and heart and lung illnesses not previously linked to tobacco. According to Dr. Graham A. Colditz of the Washington University School of Medicine, the results indicate that public health officials have seriously underestimated the effect of smoking and have not been providing smokers with the help they need to quit.

The 42 million US smokers have death rates two to three times higher than those of nonsmokers, and they die more than ten years earlier. The study showed that twice as many smokers as nonsmokers died from kidney disease, infections, and heart and respiratory illnesses not previously linked to tobacco use.

The Health Consequences of Smoking — 50 Years of Progress

In 2014, US Health and Human Services secretary Kathleen Sebelius spoke at a ceremony announcing the release of a report that examines progress in studying the health effects of tobacco.

They were six times more likely to die of intestinal illness caused by inadequate blood flow.[6] According to Brian D. Carter, an epidemiologist at the American Cancer Society, this evidence is very strong. First, the statistics make sense biologically. Second,

the risk of disease was directly correlated with the amount of
smoking. And third, the risk diminished in smokers who quit.

Education about the dangers of smoking has changed
people's attitudes. Smoking leads to serious health problems,
lowered workplace productivity due to illness, and higher

HOW THE CDC FIGHTS SMOKING

The CDC's most successful campaign to discourage smoking is the "Tips From Former Smokers" campaign, introduced in 2012. The ads show real smokers dealing with the diseases resulting from their smoking addiction. For example, a woman named Terrie started smoking in high school. She contracted oral and throat cancer at age 40, and doctors removed her larynx. The ad shows her after cancer had ravaged her face and body. Terrie died of smoking-related cancer at age 53. A user comment on a CDC Facebook page reacts to Terrie's ad and the Tips campaign:

> I am 41 years old and have smoked a pack a day for 26 years. I always knew I needed to quit. I can barely breathe and my heart races at the slightest movement. I am now for the first time in 26 years smokefree. I thank you for those scary commercials, and I thank Terrie for allowing her story to be told. I quit and I owe it to her.[7]

insurance rates because of the expensive treatments required for smoking-caused diseases. These factors have caused people to become less accepting of smokers. The number of people quitting smoking in the United States has begun rising. Those who quit tend to be older, and tobacco companies have responded by targeting their advertising to young adults and teenagers.

As understanding of the adverse health effects of smoking has risen in the developed countries of North America and Western Europe, smoking has declined. But tobacco companies have not given up. In addition to young people, they have set their sights on the world's developing nations in Africa, Asia, the Middle East, the former Soviet Union,

Representatives from cigarette companies distributed their products at roadside shops in Burma in 2013.

and Latin America. These countries have few or no smoking regulations, making it easier to target potential smokers, both teens and adults. Current trends suggest that by 2020, ten million people per year will die from tobacco use around the world. Seventy percent of these deaths will occur in developing nations.[8]

CHAPTER FOUR

TOBACCO AND CANCER

Cancer can begin in almost any cell in the body. All cancers are related, and all have one basic characteristic: some of the body's cells begin to divide without control. In healthy cells, the process of cell division, or mitosis, is highly controlled. It happens on a strict schedule during growth and when the body is replacing aging or injured cells. In mitosis, the cell's DNA duplicates, and the cell divides to form two identical daughter cells. Cells in different body tissues replace themselves at different rates. Skin cells divide rapidly, liver cells much more slowly.

In cancer, control of mitosis breaks down, and cells reproduce too rapidly. They usually form solid masses, or tumors. Cancer

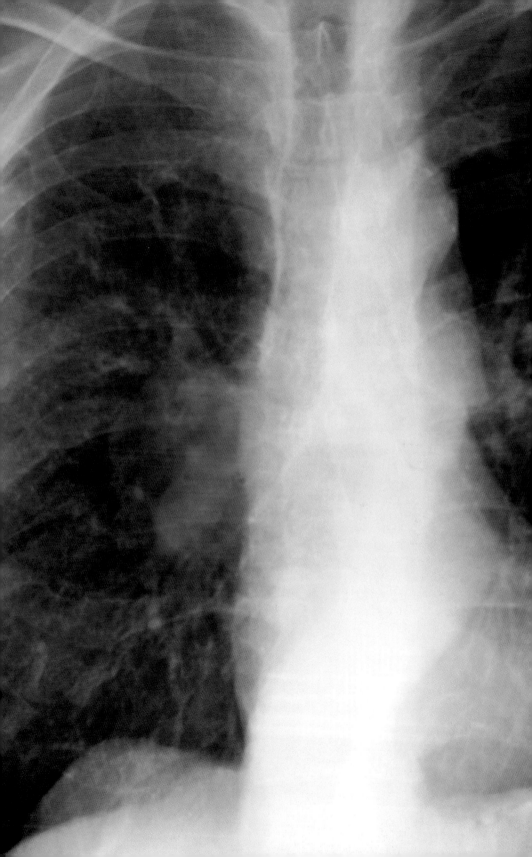

cells are malignant, meaning they invade other tissues. They may get around the body's immune system or make it work on their behalf. Cancer cells are less specialized than normal cells. They lose their normal function. Cancerous lung cells no longer carry out lung functions. They take over nearby cells and make them serve the tumor—for example, cancer cells can cause the body to form blood vessels that supply the growing tumor with nutrients and oxygen and remove its waste.

The causes of cancer vary. It is genetic in the sense that it involves changes, or mutations, in a cell's genetic material. The genetic defect may be inherited, or it may occur when cells are damaged due to exposure to some environmental factor, often radiation or chemicals. Tobacco, with its vast assortment of carcinogens, is a major cancer-causing agent.

HOW CANCER SPREADS

At the primary site, where a cancer begins, the cancer forms fingerlike projections that invade surrounding healthy tissue. Sometimes cells break off from the primary cancer and enter the bloodstream. Most of these cells die, destroyed by immune cells in the blood. Those that settle in other parts of the body can grow new tumors. The cancer is now metastatic. When a lung cancer forms a new tumor elsewhere in the body, it is referred to as metastatic lung cancer.

LUNG CANCER

Lung cancer is caused by gene mutations in the DNA of lung cells. Cigarette smoke contains many mutagens, including benzopyrene, carbon monoxide, and hydrogen peroxide. The first research into causes of lung cancer began in 1948, when Ernst Wynder, a medical student at Washington University in Saint Louis, Missouri, observed the blackened lungs of a lung cancer victim. Wynder later published a study showing increased rates of lung cancer in smokers versus nonsmokers. In 1998, researchers found that benzopyrene shut off the action of a gene called p53. This gene's job is to ensure that healthy cells divide, while unhealthy ones die. Shutting it off allows cancer cells to divide and spread.

Sometimes smoking does not specifically cause lung cancer, but instead enables it. Smoking weakens the lungs and irritates the respiratory passages. This makes it difficult for the body to remove particles from the lungs, making the lungs more susceptible to other carcinogens. For example, exposure to both cigarette smoke and the carcinogen asbestos increases the likelihood of lung cancer by 40 times, compared to those who smoke and have no exposure to asbestos.[1]

"Lung cancer is the leading cause of cancer death for both men and women."[4]

—Centers for Disease Control and Prevention

Around the world, approximately 1.2 million people die of lung cancer every year.[2] In 2017, an estimated 155,870 of these deaths occurred in the United States.[3] Eighty to 90 percent of US lung cancer deaths were related to cigarette smoking. Smoking cigarettes increases a person's risk for lung cancer by 15 to

Comparing a healthy lung, *left*, with a smoker's lung, *right*, makes tobacco's devastation apparent.

30 times. The chance of contracting lung cancer rises with the number of cigarettes smoked per day and the number of years a person has smoked. Smoking pipes or cigars also increases the risk. Quitting smoking lowers the risk, but it is never again as low as the risk for nonsmokers.

OTHER CANCERS CAUSED BY TOBACCO

Lung cancer is the most common tobacco-related cancer, and it causes the most deaths. But at least 14 kinds of cancers are related to tobacco use, and they occur throughout the body. Besides lung cancer, tobacco use causes cancers of the mouth and throat, esophagus, stomach, colon and rectum, liver, pancreas, larynx, trachea, bronchus, kidney, bladder, and cervix. It also causes a blood cancer, acute myeloid leukemia.

Approximately 40 percent of all US cancers diagnosed, and 30 percent of all cancer deaths, are related to tobacco use. Lung, colon, and rectal cancer together account for more than one-half of all tobacco-related cancers.[5]

Smokeless tobacco, which includes chewing tobacco and snuff, contains at least 28 carcinogens. Some people use smokeless tobacco because they think it is safer than smoking. It is not. Lung cancer is less likely because the tobacco is not inhaled. But toxins are still taken in through the mucous membranes of the mouth and throat, making these areas prime targets for cancer. Smokeless tobacco is a major cause of oral, esophageal, and pancreatic cancers. And, like all forms of tobacco, it contains nicotine— often in higher concentrations than in cigarettes—so it is addictive.

The good news is that tobacco-related cancer deaths are decreasing in the United

WHY CANCERS ARE DIFFERENT

There are more than 100 kinds of cancer. They are usually named for the type of tissue or organ in which they originate. Characteristics of cancer cells vary, depending on their origin. Carcinomas occur in epithelial cells, those that make up the skin and linings inside the body. Squamous (flat) epithelial cells line organs including the stomach, intestines, lungs, bladder, and kidneys. Squamous cell carcinomas affect these organs. Sarcomas form in bone and in soft tissues such as muscle, fat, blood and lymph vessels, as well as in tendons and ligaments. Leukemia begins in the blood-forming cells of the bone marrow. Lymphoma begins in lymphocytes, the immune cells that fight infections.

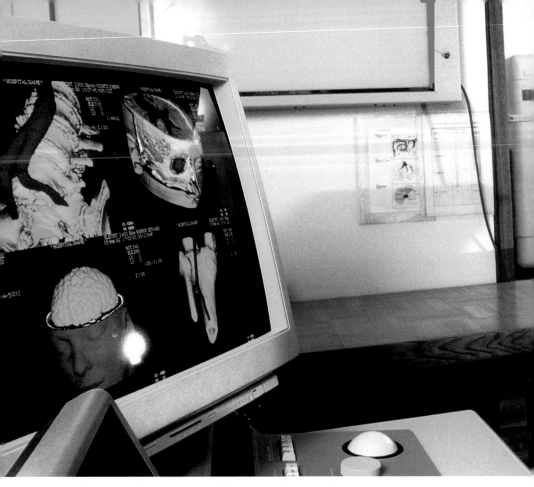

Computed tomography (CT) scans, which use X-ray images and intense computer processing, peer inside the body and can reveal the presence of cancers.

States. Between 1990 and 2016, the United States avoided about 1.3 million cancer deaths.[6] This decline was due to earlier detection, advances in treatments, and comprehensive programs for both tobacco and cancer control. The CDC funds 65 programs aimed at decreasing tobacco-related cancers. The programs create tobacco-free environments. They increase access to early cancer detection and care programs for tobacco users. They sponsor programs to help smokers quit. Finally, they concentrate

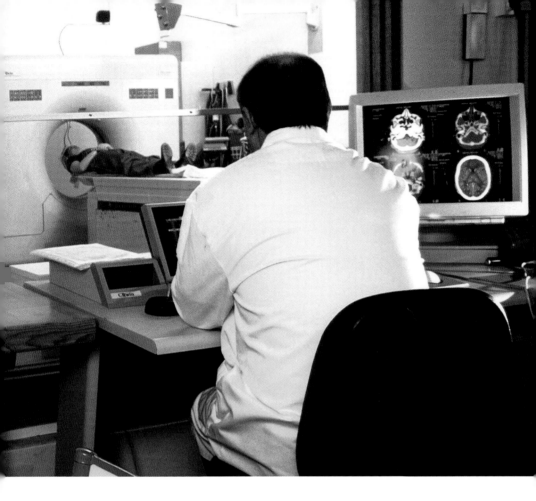

on improving cancer outcomes in communities with particularly high rates of tobacco-related cancers and deaths.

DETECTING AND TREATING TOBACCO-CAUSED CANCERS

The best way to avoid tobacco-caused cancers is to not use tobacco. Smokers should quit immediately. Smokers

Smoking one cigarette shortens a person's life by 10 minutes; smoking a pack shortens it 3.5 hours. A two-pack-per-day smoker loses more than 100 days of life each year.[7]

should receive cancer screenings, which could help catch cancers early, while they are still curable. Lung cancer screenings are done by a process called Low-Dose Computed Tomography (LDCT). LDCT is recommended for people aged 55 to 80 who smoke at least 30 packs of cigarettes per year. People who have not smoked for 15 years or more can discontinue screenings. Screenings for cervical and colorectal cancers are also effective for early diagnoses.

Cancer treatments depend on a person's health, the stage of the cancer, and personal preference. Types of treatments include surgery, chemotherapy, radiation therapy, and targeted drug therapy. Sometimes a combination is used. Surgery involves removing the section of the organ (say, a lung) containing the tumor, plus a region of healthy tissue surrounding it. Lymph nodes may be examined to check them for cancer spread. Chemotherapy uses drugs, sometimes in combination, to kill cancer cells. It may be used alone or after surgery to kill any remaining cancer

CHANCES OF SURVIVING TOBACCO-CAUSED CANCERS

Cancer survival rates tell the chances of a person surviving a certain type of cancer for a given time period, usually five years. For example, the five-year survival rate for bladder cancer is 78 percent. That is, for every 100 people diagnosed with bladder cancer, 78 will still be alive in five years.[8] Of the types of cancer caused by tobacco use, five have very low five-year survival rates: pancreatic (8.5%), liver (18.1%), lung (18.7%), esophageal (20.5%), and stomach (31.1%).[9]

cells. Targeted drug therapy involves using drugs against certain characteristics of cancer cells, such as specific gene mutations. Radiation treatments may be used for small tumors or tumors that cannot be removed surgically.

Tobacco-related cancers are a major health problem in the United States, and lung cancer—the major tobacco-caused cancer—is one of the hardest cancers to treat. But tobacco is also the number one cause of preventable death and cancer death in the United States. Many of these deaths can be stopped. People who quit using tobacco will very likely live longer than if they keep using it.

BENEFITS OF QUITTING SMOKING

Benefits from quitting smoking begin almost immediately. After only 20 minutes, the ex-smoker's heart rate and blood pressure decline. After 12 hours, blood carbon monoxide levels drop to normal. Within two weeks to three months, circulation and lung function improve. By nine months, coughing and shortness of breath have declined. Cilia in the respiratory tract are regaining normal function. They are able to remove mucus and particles from the lungs, and infections will decrease. A year after quitting, the person's excess risk of heart disease is one-half that of a smoker. The risk of stroke can fall to that of a nonsmoker within two to five years. After five years, the risk of mouth, throat, esophageal, and bladder cancer are cut in half, and the risk of cervical cancer is as low as that of a nonsmoker. After ten years, the risk of death from lung cancer is half that of a smoker. After 15 years, the risk of coronary disease is that of a nonsmoker.[10]

CHAPTER FIVE

TOBACCO AND RESPIRATORY DISEASE

The human respiratory system breathes in oxygen-rich air and breathes out waste carbon dioxide. Air enters through the nose, which opens into the mouth and into a series of linked air cavities, the nasal sinuses. This region warms and moistens the air. The cilia and mucus in the nose and throat trap dangerous particles and keep them from entering

The respiratory system is particularly vulnerable to the chemicals found in tobacco smoke.

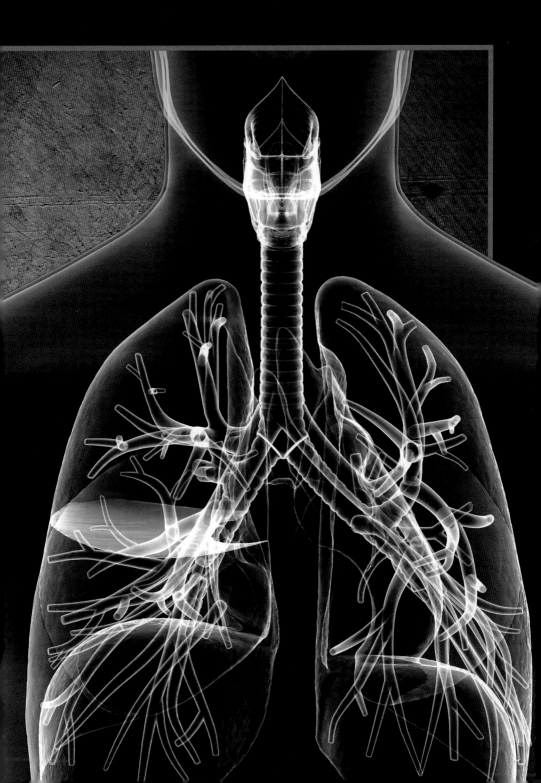

the lungs. Particles include dust, smoke, bacteria, viruses, and allergy-causing substances, among others. But particles of cigarette smoke damage and paralyze the cilia, preventing them from doing their job.

Warmed air passes from the mouth and sinuses through the larynx (voice box) and trachea (windpipe). The end of the trachea branches to form two bronchial tubes, or bronchi, which enter the two lungs. As the bronchi advance into the lungs, they branch more and more, eventually forming bronchioles that end in tiny balloon-like air sacs, or alveoli. The alveoli are only a single cell thick, and they lie next to tiny blood vessels called capillaries. Air passes between the alveoli and capillaries, with oxygen entering the blood and carbon dioxide entering the alveoli, where it can be breathed out. The treelike complexes of branching tubes, alveoli, and associated blood vessels are surrounded by membranes. Together, these structures form the lungs.

EFFECTS OF SMOKING ON RESPIRATORY RATE

Respiratory rate is the number of breaths per minute taken by a person at rest. Smoking impacts breathing by paralyzing cilia, which become clogged with tar. The lining of the entire respiratory tract becomes inflamed and thickened, narrowing air passages. Smoking deteriorates elastin, an elastic protein in the lungs, making it more difficult to breathe in and out. Nicotine causes adrenaline release, which constricts the blood vessels, raises blood pressure, and increases heart rate. Together, these factors can drastically increase respiratory rates.

The lungs are divided into lobes, three in the right lung and two in the left.

It is not surprising that smoking causes respiratory problems. Each time smokers inhale cigarette smoke, they are inhaling a huge hit of toxic air pollution that damages all parts of the respiratory system.

RESPIRATORY IRRITATIONS

Smoking damage to the respiratory system begins with the first puff, as the smoke slows the motion of cilia in the nose, trachea, bronchi, and bronchioles. The cilia lose their ability to clean the air entering the lungs. Mucus and tar from the smoke begin to build up, irritating the respiratory lining. Mucus production increases, and the lining of the bronchioles thickens, further clogging the system. As smoking continues, constant irritation of the respiratory tract and loss of ciliary action leads to chronic bronchitis, or inflammation of the bronchi. The smoker develops a distinctive, persistent cough. The cough is necessary

SMOKING STUNTS LUNG GROWTH

People who start smoking as teenagers can limit their future potential. Teenagers' lungs are still growing, and chemicals in cigarette smoke slow the rate of lung growth. The lungs of teen smokers may never reach their full adult size or be able to perform at their full capacity. This can decrease a smoker's ability to participate in active physical activities, such as running, swimming, or competitive sports.

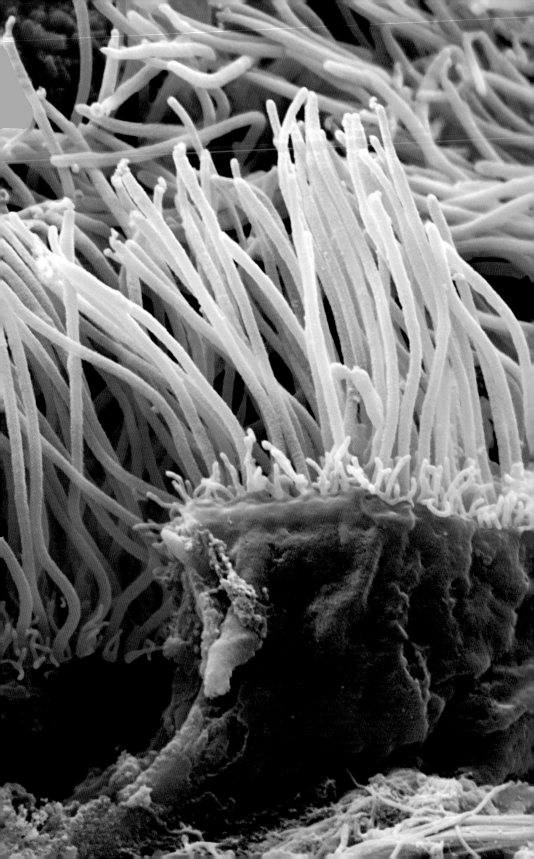

to rid the lungs of mucus, since the cilia are no longer functional. Bronchioles also become less elastic, making breathing more difficult. Eventually, labored breathing begins to cause alveoli to explode, and the irreversible damage leading to a condition called emphysema has begun. At the same time, changes to the lung cells may be occurring that could lead to lung cancer.

Rhinitis is an inflammation of the membranes of the nose, and sinusitis is an inflammation of the sinus cavities. Both are typical conditions of smokers that happen when the cilia are damaged. Rhinitis has symptoms similar to the common cold, including sneezing, congestion, runny nose, and itchy nose, eyes, and ears. Sinusitis has these symptoms, plus headaches, facial pain and swelling, and a decreased sense of smell. It is more serious and harder to get rid of than a cold, and it may become chronic. Asthma is also more common in smokers, both teens and adults.

DEATH BY TOBACCO

Chronic obstructive pulmonary disease (COPD) is defined to include chronic bronchitis, emphysema, or both. COPD is the third-leading cause of death in the United States, after heart disease and cancer.

"I am not yet using oxygen, but I know that day will come. I am unable to do many of the things I love. I cannot dance. I cannot do my own food shopping. I cannot take long walks along the river at sunset with my husband."[1]

—Elaine L. Ackley, 58 years old, COPD patient

In 2014, it killed more than 155,000 Americans.[2] Worldwide, in 2015, it killed an estimated three million people, more than 90 percent of them in low- and middle-income countries. COPD develops slowly and is usually not noticed until a person is 40 to 50 years old. In coming years, there will likely be more cases of COPD, as populations age and smoking increases in less-developed countries.

The inability of cilia to remove foreign particles means that more bacteria and viruses enter the lungs and remain there. This makes smokers more likely to get respiratory infections, such as colds and flu. They are more vulnerable to serious diseases such as pneumonia and tuberculosis, too. Smoking also damages the immune system, so infections last longer and cause more damage. Doctors think these repeated infections may be one factor leading to COPD.

LUNG FUNCTION IN PIPE AND CIGAR SMOKERS

Two lung function tests are used on people with COPD. Forced expiratory volume in one second (FEV1) tests how much air a person can forcefully exhale in one second. Forced vital capacity (FVC) tests how much air a person can forcefully exhale after taking a deep breath. A study including cigar and pipe smokers found decreased lung function even in those who had never smoked a cigarette. Compared to nonsmokers, pipe smokers showed decreased FEV1 values and cigar smokers showed decreased FVC values. Both showed increased likelihood of airflow obstruction.

COPD is progressive, meaning it worsens and grows as time goes on. It is ultimately fatal. It begins with chronic bronchitis, which makes breathing difficult by narrowing the bronchi and filling them with mucus. As smoking continues, the tiny bronchioles and alveoli become less elastic. It is harder to push air out of the lungs, and air collects there. Consequently, less air can be breathed in. Thus, the key features of early COPD are shortness of breath and a chronic, mucus-producing cough.

As stress on the alveoli increases and pressure builds up because air cannot be breathed out, the alveoli fill up and eventually begin to explode, decreasing the lung surface area. The person's condition has now progressed to emphysema. Air from the burst alveoli cannot be breathed out, and it collects in the lung cavities. Destroyed air sacs cannot be replaced. As more alveoli break, the person's lung capacity decreases and less oxygen-containing air is breathed in. This causes weakness and difficulty doing even simple daily activities. Emphysema sufferers also experience what are known as exacerbations. These episodes last several days or weeks. They involve increased levels of breathlessness, coughing, and mucus production. Exacerbations may require hospitalization.

TREATING EMPHYSEMA AND COPD

Emphysema cannot be cured, but treatment can slow its progression. The cheapest, most effective treatment is to stop smoking. This slows down the progression of symptoms and decreases the chance of a COPD-related death. Maintaining a healthy lifestyle can also help. This includes avoiding smoke and air pollution that irritate the lungs, using an air filter in the home, getting as much exercise as possible, and eating well to maintain a healthy weight.

Several medications can help, too. Bronchodilators relax constricted airways, and they can relieve symptoms such as shortness of breath and coughing. Corticosteroid drugs inhaled as aerosol sprays can reduce inflammation and relieve shortness of breath. Antibiotics may be prescribed to treat bacterial infections associated with COPD. In especially severe cases of emphysema, a doctor may recommend surgery. Lung volume reduction surgery removes the most damaged sections of the lung. The remaining lung tissue can then expand and work more efficiently. In more severe cases, a lung transplant may be recommended.

In short, smoking destroys lung tissue, and once destroyed, the tissue cannot be replaced. As the number of cigarettes smoked per day and the number of years of smoking increase, lung damage increases. But all smoking causes damage. The only sure way to keep the respiratory system healthy is not to smoke at all.

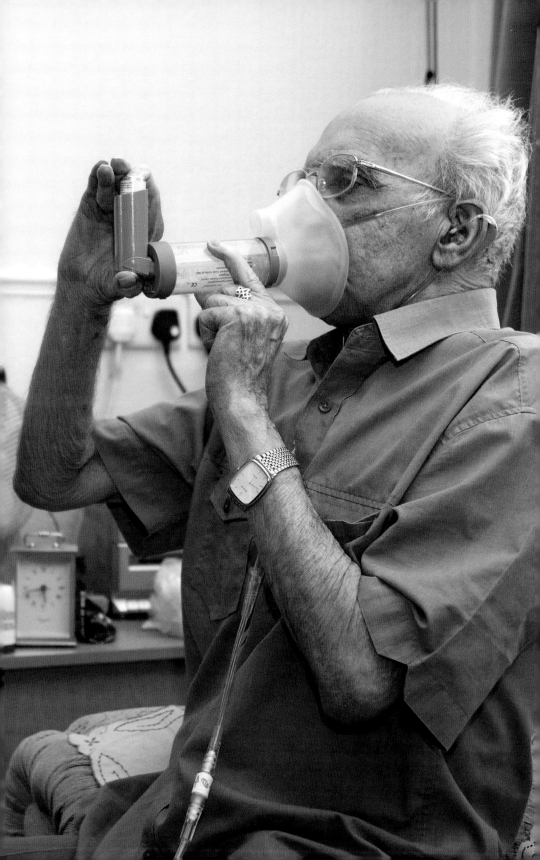

CHAPTER SIX

TOBACCO AND CIRCULATORY DISEASE

The circulatory system includes the heart, blood, and blood vessels. It is also called the cardiovascular system. Blood pumped by the heart and carried through the blood vessels delivers gases and nutrients to all body cells. It also removes waste from the cells. Arteries carry blood away from the heart; veins return it. The largest artery, the aorta, branches into smaller arteries and arterioles, and then into tiny capillaries, which form networks throughout the body. Arterial capillaries feed into venous

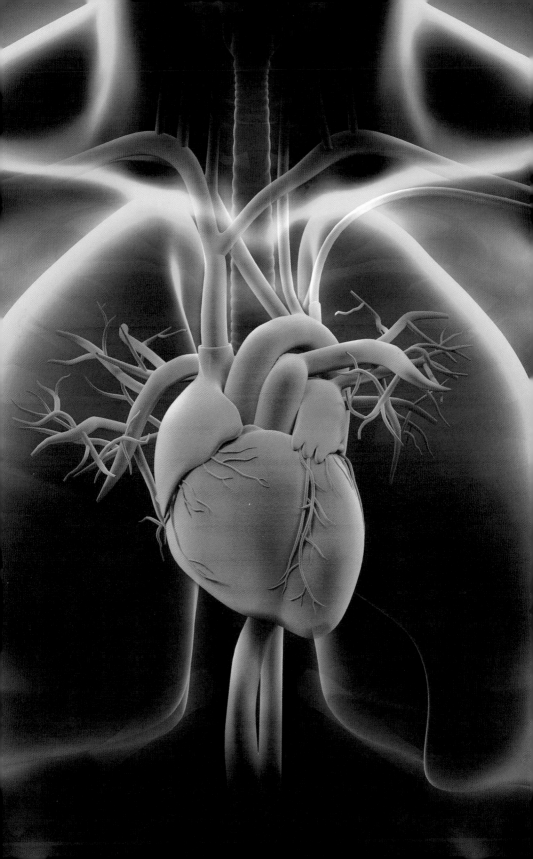

capillaries, which combine to form successively larger veins, which eventually return blood to the heart. The capillary beds, or networks of arterial and venous capillaries, are the sites of gas and nutrient exchange throughout the body.

The direct connection between tobacco and respiratory disease is obvious—people breathe in tobacco smoke, which contains toxic substances. But how does tobacco affect the circulatory system? It decreases blood flow to the heart and body tissues. This deprives them of oxygen and slows healing. It increases the likelihood of blood clots, which makes heart attacks and strokes more likely. It damages the lining of blood vessels, including those in the heart.

HOW TOBACCO CAUSES CARDIOVASCULAR DISEASE

Cardiovascular disease includes diseases of the heart and blood vessels. Most cardiovascular diseases are caused by atherosclerosis, or the buildup of plaque on the arterial walls. Plaque is composed of fat, cholesterol, calcium, and other substances in the blood. As it builds up and hardens, it narrows arteries throughout the body. This slows blood flow and allows less oxygen to reach body cells. Smoking speeds up the formation of plaque and ultimately the process of atherosclerosis.

With the first puff, smoking begins to affect the heart and circulation. Nicotine causes the body to produce adrenaline and constricts blood vessels, which raises blood pressure and causes the heart to work harder. Because blood vessels are narrowed, less oxygen can reach body cells. The carbon monoxide in tobacco smoke attaches to hemoglobin, the oxygen-carrying molecule in red blood cells. With the carbon monoxide in the way, fewer oxygen molecules can attach to hemoglobin, reducing the amount of oxygen available to body cells.

Smoking stimulates blood clotting by raising levels of a clotting protein called fibrinogen. This causes platelets, the blood cell fragments involved in clotting, to stick together. The result is an increased likelihood of clots that could cause a heart attack (blockage of arteries near the heart) or stroke (blockage of arteries in the brain). Smoking increases blood cholesterol levels, another risk factor for cardiovascular disease. These factors all increase the

BAN SMOKING, CUT HEART ATTACKS

A study analyzed 45 smoking bans, including 33 in US cities and states and others in Germany, New Zealand, and other countries. After laws banned smoking in public places, such as restaurants, bars, and workplaces, heart attack hospitalizations dropped an average of 15 percent and stroke hospitalizations dropped 16 percent. The more complete the ban (the more places it included), the greater the effect. A 2002 smoking ban in restaurants in Olmsted County, Minnesota, had no effect on heart attack rates. However, expanding the ban to all bars and workplaces in the county in 2007 decreased heart attacks by 33 percent.[1]

rate at which atherosclerosis develops. Thus, smoking works in multiple ways to damage the circulatory system.

TOBACCO AND RISK FACTORS

The risk for smoking-related cardiovascular disease is real. In the United States, 480,000 people per year die from smoking-related diseases. One in five of these deaths is caused by heart disease. Compared to nonsmokers, cigarette smokers are two to four times more likely to get heart disease, and twice as likely to have a stroke. Another 34,000 people per year die just from being exposed to secondhand, or environmental, smoke.[2] That is, they don't smoke themselves but spend time around people who do. Secondhand smoke is especially dangerous for pregnant women, infants, and young children.

There are six independent risk factors for coronary or peripheral artery disease that

CORONARY ARTERY DISEASE

When atherosclerosis affects the coronary arteries, the arteries that supply the heart, it is called coronary artery disease. Coronary artery disease includes angina and heart attacks. Angina is chest pain caused when the heart does not receive enough oxygen. A heart attack results from complete blockage of the coronary arteries by a blood clot. A heart attack may cause permanent damage to the heart muscle or even death. Atherosclerosis affecting arteries outside the heart is peripheral artery disease. Complete blockage of arteries leading to the brain is a stroke, which kills or damages brain cells. Depending on which brain region is affected, the person can suffer damage to mind or body functions, such as paralysis or loss of speech or memory.

people can control. They are cigarette smoking, high cholesterol, high blood pressure, physical activity, obesity, and diabetes. Smoking is the most important risk factor for young men and women. Smokers under 40 are five times more likely to have heart attacks than nonsmokers of the same age. The earlier a person starts smoking, the more likely that person will die of cardiovascular disease. A long-term British study showed that the death rate due to cardiovascular disease was twice as high in smokers as in nonsmokers. The difference was even greater in middle-aged people.

If smoking is combined with even one other risk factor, such as obesity or low physical activity, the risk of cardiovascular disease, heart attack, or stroke is much greater. The same is true for anyone with a family history of heart disease.

CIGARS AND HEART DISEASE

Cigars, like cigarettes, damage the heart and circulatory system. Smoking cigars increases the risk of both heart disease and stroke, raising the risk of early death from heart disease by 30 percent.[3] In addition to circulatory effects, cigar smokers have higher death rates from COPD and from cancers of the throat, mouth, lips, larynx, and esophagus than nonsmokers. Former US surgeon general David Satcher argues, "It's critical that cigars not be (seen) as a safe or less costly alternative to cigarettes."[4]

"In the USA, the majority of smokers do not believe they have a greater risk of heart disease than nonsmokers."[5]

—*World Heart Federation*

Every year in the United States, more than 170,000 women die of smoking-related diseases. Many additional women die from using smokeless tobacco. At one time, men were far more likely to die of tobacco use than women, but that has changed. The overall risk for women is now approximately equal to that for men. In the United States, women smokers over 35 have a slightly higher risk than men of dying from coronary heart disease.[6]

In short, smoking is extremely damaging to the heart and blood vessels. Smoking is a major risk factor for cardiovascular diseases, and it causes or contributes to nearly every type of circulatory-related disease. Long-term smoking can lead to death due to any of these types of cardiovascular disease, and the greater the amount of smoking, the more likely it will lead to a fatal cardiovascular disease.

CHAPTER SEVEN

TOBACCO AND OTHER HEALTH PROBLEMS

Tobacco use affects all body systems, causing serious illness and death due to respiratory diseases, circulatory diseases, and cancers. Tobacco also ravages the human body in ways that do not necessarily kill, but almost always lower the smoker's quality of life. These include effects on pregnancy, skin and aging, the mouth and teeth, and stamina and overall health.

Smoking while pregnant can have a serious effect on the health of the child.

REPORTS ON HEALTH EFFECTS

In 1962, the United Kingdom's Royal College of Physicians published a report titled "Smoking and Health." The report connected smoking to several diseases and conditions, including lung cancer. At the time, smoking was socially accepted and few people took its dangers seriously. In the United Kingdom, 70 percent of men and 40 percent of women smoked. Fifty years later, in 2012, the percentage of smokers had decreased to only 21 percent of men and women. Smokers as a group had changed from affluent to poor. The public had become more aware of tobacco's effect on health. Smoking was less accepted. One female smoker explained, "I'm not proud of it. I won't encourage my children to do it—I go outside at home."[2]

TOBACCO AND PREGNANCY

Smoking during pregnancy, or being around secondhand smoke, puts both mother and baby at risk. If the mother breathes in smoke, chemicals from the smoke, including nicotine and carbon monoxide, are transferred to the baby across the placenta. These chemicals decrease the baby's oxygen and nutrient supply. Smoking doubles the risk of the mother having abnormal bleeding during pregnancy and birth. The placental membranes can rupture prematurely. Smoking can even lead to miscarriage or stillbirth.

Babies born to smoking mothers are more likely to be premature, or born three weeks or more before the due date. These babies miss important growth milestones that occur in the last weeks of pregnancy, and they are more likely to have serious health problems. They can suffer breathing problems, feeding problems, cerebral palsy, developmental delays, or problems with eyesight or hearing. Smoking slows growth, so babies are often underweight. Smokers' babies may suffer from brain development problems, and they have a higher risk of dying from Sudden Infant Death Syndrome (SIDS), the unexplained death of a seemingly healthy baby.

SMOKING MOTHERS AND BIRTH DEFECTS

The risk of low-birth-weight babies, premature births, and miscarriages in mothers who smoke is well known. Additionally, these babies have a higher risk of birth defects. Smokers' babies are 26 percent more likely than nonsmokers' babies to have missing or deformed limbs, 28 percent more likely to have a clubfoot or cleft lip, and 33 percent more likely to have skull defects. A condition in which the stomach or intestine protrudes through the skin is 50 percent more likely. These statistics are based on 174,000 cases of malformations occurring from 1959 to 2010.[3]

For their own health and that of their babies, women who are pregnant or planning to become pregnant should not smoke. Quitting smoking before pregnancy is best, but quitting at any time during pregnancy will help the baby's chances. Some women stop smoking during pregnancy but relapse after the birth, sometimes due to the stress of new motherhood. If this happens, the mother should not smoke around the baby. If the mother continues smoking and breastfeeds, the baby will receive chemicals from the smoke through the breast milk.

TOBACCO AND THE MOUTH

Tobacco use affects the appearance and cleanliness of the mouth. The chemicals in the smoke cause bad breath and discolor the teeth. The openings of the salivary glands in the roof of the mouth may become inflamed in response to these chemicals. These effects make the mouth tissues more susceptible to bacteria. When bacteria are not cleaned from the teeth, they form a film called plaque, which hardens to form tartar. Gum disease begins when bacteria from the teeth get between the teeth and gums, causing an infection called gingivitis. If gingivitis is left untreated, the gums may begin to separate from the teeth, and infections form in the spaces. This more severe condition is gum disease. Eventually, the bones in the gums can break down, causing the teeth to loosen. At this point, the teeth may need to be pulled.

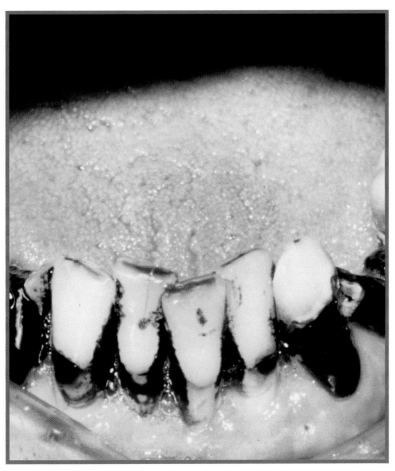

Over time, smoking can cause dangerous, painful conditions of the teeth and gums.

Smokers are twice as likely to get gum disease as nonsmokers. The more they smoke, and the longer they smoke, the greater their likelihood of getting gum disease. Smoking aggravates gum disease because of its effect on the immune system. A smoker's body is less able to fight off gum infections. Infections also take longer to heal, so treatments may not work as well. Overall, smoking may be the greatest preventable risk for gum diseases. More than one-half of chronic cases of gum disease in the United States result from cigarette smoking.[4]

TOBACCO AND AGING

Smoking causes premature aging, which is most clearly seen in the skin. The narrowing of blood vessels slows blood flow to the skin. This decreases the amount of oxygen and nutrients that the skin receives. Other chemicals in tobacco smoke damage elastin and collagen, the proteins that make skin strong and elastic. This causes the skin to age more rapidly, resulting in wrinkling and sagging. This is most obvious on the skin, but it occurs throughout the body. The aging effect of smoking may be overlooked because it is not visible at first. However, wrinkling and other signs of aging, once they have happened, cannot be reversed. The more a person smokes, and the longer he or she continues, the worse the damage becomes. Because e-cigarettes contain

DOES SMOKING RUIN YOUR LOOKS?

Smoking can devastate a person's appearance. The most obvious changes occur in the hair, nails, and skin. Smoking causes more rapid hair graying and hair loss. It increases fungal infections in the fingernails and toenails. Skin is loose, sagging, and wrinkled, as are certain areas of the body, such as the breasts and upper arms. There are lines and wrinkles around the lips, mouth, and eyes. Skin tone is uneven, and age spots appear more frequently and at a younger age. Stained teeth, nails, and fingers are common. Smoking increases the risk of having the skin condition psoriasis, which causes scaly, dry rashes.

nicotine and other harmful chemicals, including carcinogens, these aging effects, including wrinkles, will still occur if a person uses e-cigarettes.

Researchers may have discovered how smoking affects aging. A rare genetic defect called Werner syndrome causes very rapid aging. As young as their twenties, people with Werner syndrome get gray hair, thinner skin, and hoarse voices. Soon after, they develop other conditions of aging, including cataracts, diabetes, atherosclerosis, and weak bones. In their forties and fifties, they die of diseases of the elderly, including cancer and heart disease. People with Werner syndrome have a defect in the WRN gene. This gene makes the protein WRN, which protects and repairs DNA in body cells. Werner sufferers make too little WRN, so their body cells age too rapidly. Smoking has the exact same effect. It also causes cells to produce less WRN, so the cells of smokers age too rapidly. Researchers hope this new discovery of the connection between the WRN mutation and smoking will lead to treatments for smoking-related conditions.

Even if the effects of smoking were not life-threatening, the changes it causes in everyday life and appearance should be enough to cause most people to think twice before beginning to smoke—or if they already smoke, to give it up. Evidence shows that not smoking will result in a longer, healthier, and more rewarding life.

CHAPTER EIGHT

SOCIAL AND LEGAL IMPLICATIONS

Some people consider smoking a personal issue. They assume their smoking is no one else's business—it harms no one but them. But, of the more than seven million people who die every year from tobacco-related illnesses, approximately 890,000 of them die from exposure to secondhand smoke.[1] This factor, along with medical and business costs, makes smoking not just a personal problem, but also a social and legal one.

SMOKING AND DOLLARS

In 2015, 15.1 percent of US adults, or 36.5 million people, smoked. This included 16.7 percent of males and 13.6 percent of females.[2] Smoking takes a major toll on the US economy. Every year, the United States spends almost $170 billion on medical care for adults suffering from tobacco-related illnesses. Businesses lose more than $156 billion per year due to lower productivity caused by health problems, premature deaths, and exposure to secondhand smoke.[3] A study by the Ohio State University showed that a smoker costs an employer almost $6,000 per year more than a nonsmoker, due to smoke breaks, skipping work, and extra health care.[4]

A 2016 study from the University of California San Francisco showed that when smoking rates decline, health-care costs drop steeply. A 10 percent smoking decline in the United States would result in a reduction of $63 billion in total health-care costs the following year. Costs decline because risks for smoking-related diseases, such as heart attack and stroke, drop by approximately one-half in the first year after a smoker quits. Similar drops occur for other diseases. An earlier study showed these declines for California and Arizona. The new study extended the findings to all 50 states and the District of Columbia. According to coauthor Stanton A. Glantz, "These findings show that state and national policies that reduce smoking not only will improve health, but can be a key part of health care cost containment even in the short run."[6]

THE COST OF SMOKING

A 2013 study at the Ohio State University found that, on average, every smoker costs his or her employer $5,816 per year. The largest proportion, $3,077, is due to work time lost to smoking breaks—an average of five daily breaks, compared to the three typically allowed. The second highest proportion, $2,056, results from higher health-care costs, because smokers have more serious illnesses.[7] Remaining costs result from smokers missing more workdays than nonsmokers, and having generally lower productivity due to health problems. The researchers suggested companies could lower costs by sponsoring programs to stop smoking.

SECONDHAND SMOKE

When someone smokes a tobacco product—a cigarette, cigar, or pipe—most of the

"Smoking costs the United States billions of dollars each year."[8]

—*Centers for Disease Control and Prevention*

smoke does not enter the lungs, and the person exhales some of the smoke that was inhaled. This smoke enters the environment and is breathed in by people nearby. This secondhand smoke includes the same toxic chemicals inhaled by the primary smoker and is just as dangerous. People can be exposed to secondhand smoke almost everywhere, including homes, workplaces, bars, restaurants, and cars. Most exposure happens in homes and workplaces.

People who breathe secondhand smoke contract the same tobacco-related diseases as smokers. Between 1964 and 2016, approximately 2.5 million Americans died from exposure to secondhand smoke.[9] Every year, about 3,000 nonsmokers die of lung cancer due to exposure to secondhand smoke. According to the surgeon general, a person who lives with a smoker has a 20 to 30 percent greater chance of getting lung cancer than they would otherwise. The risk of heart disease increases by 25 to 30 percent, and secondhand smoke kills about 46,000 people every year due to heart disease.[10] There is no safe level of secondhand smoke for children or adults. The only way to be safe from secondhand smoke is to eliminate smoking in homes, workplaces, and other public areas.

An emerging issue centers around what is known as thirdhand smoke. This consists of the residue left behind on clothes and indoor surfaces after a person has smoked in an area. When people touch these surfaces or breathe nearby, they can take nicotine and other chemicals from tobacco into their bodies. Thorough cleaning is needed to permanently remove these residues. Research is still being done on the potential dangers of thirdhand smoke.

TOBACCO LAWS

Tobacco control laws and regulations are designed to improve public health by preventing people from starting tobacco use, helping tobacco users quit, and reducing the harmful effects of tobacco use. As evidence for the health dangers of tobacco products built up, the United States began to develop comprehensive plans to limit disease and deaths due to tobacco. An important part of these plans was the development of laws and regulations.

"The costs imposed by tobacco use are not simply financial costs. It is not possible to put a price on the lost lives and the human suffering caused by smoking."[11]

—Micah Berman and colleagues, Ohio State University

Federal tobacco regulation began in 1966 with the first warnings on US cigarette packages. Since then, warning labels have spread around the world, with a strong boost from WHO's 2003 Framework Convention on Tobacco Control. As of 2016, 46 countries have large, graphic warning labels on their cigarette packages.[12] The labels show pictures of rotting teeth, diseased lungs, and other extreme results of smoking. The United States is not one of the countries with such labels. Although the FDA tried to institute this policy in 2012, tobacco companies sued, and courts backed them. The courts said the FDA had provided no evidence that graphic labeling would decrease smoking.

On June 22, 2009, the United States passed the Family Smoking Prevention and Tobacco Control Act, usually called the Tobacco Control Act. This law restricts the marketing and sale of tobacco to youth, requires warning labels on smokeless tobacco packages, and requires that "modified risk" claims (for example, a claim that a "light" cigarette is less harmful) be backed

German cigarette packaging features graphic labels that show the health consequences of smoking.

by evidence. It also requires that tobacco producers disclose their products' ingredients, and it allows state, local, and tribal governments to regulate tobacco. A new rule created in 2016 allowed the FDA to regulate newer products such as e-cigarettes. Mitch Zeller, director of the FDA's Center for Tobacco Products, explained the importance of this new authority: "Before this final rule, these products could be sold without any review of their ingredients, how they were made, and their potential dangers. Under this new rule, we're taking steps to protect Americans from the dangers of tobacco products, ensure these tobacco products have health warnings, and restrict sales to minors."[13]

TOBACCO BANS

In November 2014, the Westminster, Massachusetts, Board of Health proposed that the town become the first US town to ban the sale of all tobacco products, including cigarettes, e-cigarettes, cigars, and chewing tobacco. The town erupted in outrage. Five hundred people attended a town hall meeting held by the three Health Board members. The crowd was so angry that the meeting was closed, and the board members left under police protection. Only 17 percent of Westminster citizens smoke, and many consider it a disgusting habit. Part of their outrage related to possible loss of revenue by stores selling tobacco products. But most said their anger was about loss of freedom. One citizen, Nate Johnson, said, "They're just taking away everyday freedoms, little by little. This isn't about tobacco, it's about control."[14] Dr. Corey Saltin, a ban supporter, concluded, "This ban is going to happen somewhere, sometime. But probably not in Westminster."[15]

Beijing, China, launched a public smoking ban in 2015, advertising it with huge posters on the city's iconic Olympic stadium.

SMOKING BANS

Smoking bans began in the 1970s in response to 1964 and 1972 surgeon general's reports on the dangers of smoking. The Americans for Nonsmokers' Rights Foundation keeps a tally of state and local tobacco laws in the United States. As of January 2, 2018, it lists 22,661 US municipalities (including 81.6 percent of the US population) covered by smoking bans that apply to workplaces, restaurants, and/or bars.[16] These laws exist in 42 states and the District of Columbia. Some states include colleges and universities, as well as outdoor public venues, such as parks, beaches, or stadiums. Laws vary by state and locality.

The trend is for greater control over smoking in public areas. A review of 41 studies from North America, Europe, and China showed a significant decrease in children's lung problems after the initiation of smoke-free laws and increased tobacco prices. The study did not prove a cause-and-effect relationship between legal changes and a reduction in smoking-related health issues, but the authors concluded it should encourage further smoking bans. The Campaign for Tobacco-Free Kids outlines evidence that smoking bans encourage smokers to quit, reduce the number of cigarettes that continuing smokers consume, and discourage kids from beginning to smoke. All this evidence points to the conclusion that smoke-free laws are a great boon to public health.

RAISING THE
SMOKING AGE

STATES THAT HAVE RAISED THE TOBACCO AGE TO 21

STATES IN WHICH SOME CITIES OR COUNTIES HAVE RAISED THE TOBACCO AGE TO 21 (NUMBER SHOWN)

WASHINGTON

OREGON

IDAHO

MONTANA

SOUTH DAKOTA

WYOMING

NEVADA

UTAH

COLORADO
1

CALIFORNIA

ARIZONA
2

NEW MEXICO

PACIFIC OCEAN

ALASKA

HAWAII

By December 1, 2017, five states and more than 200 cities and counties in the United States had raised the age for purchasing tobacco to 21.

QUITTING SMOKING

Young people sometimes think that while others might get sick from using tobacco, they will be fine. But they are wrong. Quentin, a constant smoker, was diagnosed with renal cell carcinoma on his twenty-third birthday. He went through radiation, chemotherapy, and surgery. However, the cancer had spread through his liver and kidneys and along his spine. After ten months he could no longer walk, and liver failure was causing delusions and hallucinations. Just before he died, Quentin did not ask to see his baby daughter or his mother. He asked for a cigarette.

Sean had used chewing tobacco and snuff since he was 12. By age 18, a high school senior and track star, he was secretly using a can of snuff every day and a half. Then, he developed a sore on his tongue. It was cancer. He had surgery to remove part of his tongue, but the cancer had spread to his lymph nodes. A second surgery removed the lymph nodes, muscles, and most blood vessels in his neck. A third removed his lower jawbone and left him with feeding and breathing tubes. His final message to his friends was a written note reading, "Don't dip snuff."[1] He died at age 19.

"The cigarette is the only consumer product that kills when used as directed—half of its long-term users, in fact."[2]

—Dr. Scott Gottlieb, FDA Chief

WHY QUIT?

From ruining one's appearance to causing an early, horrible death, the effects of smoking or any other method of tobacco use should give anyone pause. Quitting leads to a longer life. It cuts the risk of heart attack and stroke. It decreases the risk of lung cancer, various other cancers, and respiratory diseases, including COPD. Problems with pregnancy will decrease. People who quit smoking will notice immediate effects, too. Their clothes and hair will not stink. They will not have bad breath. Their breathing will improve, and asthma symptoms will disappear. They will have more energy. People around the former smoker will benefit because they are no longer breathing secondhand smoke. Quitting benefits teens the most. Teens become addicted to tobacco very easily, and they have a hard time quitting. Never starting is preferable, but quitting as soon as possible is the next best thing.

Some health factors related to smoking are less well known. For example, the more people smoke, the more they snore. Long-term smokers are more likely to suffer from acid reflux, or heartburn. Smoking is also associated with serious long-term problems. The rate of mental decline in older smokers is five times higher than in nonsmokers, leading to a greater risk of Alzheimer's disease. Smokers are more likely to develop lupus, a chronic autoimmune disease that causes inflammation, pain, and tissue damage. Rheumatoid

YOUTH AND TOBACCO ADDICTION

In the United States, nearly 80 percent of smokers begin by the age of 18, and 90 percent start before leaving their teens. Every day, 2,300 children smoke their first cigarette. Approximately 350 become new daily smokers every day. Most kids smoke their first cigarette between ages 11 and 13; some are even younger. Some literally become tobacco-dependent with their first puff. According to the 2016 Monitoring the Future Study, 17.5 percent of tenth graders and 28.3 percent of high school seniors had tried smoking. About three out of four teens who start smoking continue into adulthood.[4] Many try to quit but fail.

arthritis, another autoimmune disease, depends on the presence of a specific gene, but smoking greatly increases the risk of this disease in people who have the gene. Older smokers are more prone to a degenerative eye condition called macular degeneration, which leads to blindness. Smoking is linked to thyroid disease, some colon cancers, breast cancer in women, and depression in young people.

THE COSTS OF SMOKERS' HEALTH CARE

Annual costs for cigarette smoking are approximately $65 billion per year, but smokers pay only a fraction of this. Society pays for most of it, in the form of higher insurance premiums for everyone and government expenditures such as disability benefits. People disagree on who should bear the costs. One group thinks smokers, who knowingly and voluntarily harm themselves, should pay their own costs. This group argues it is unjust to burden those who maintain healthy habits with the costs of those who do not. Also, they believe penalties for smokers, such as higher costs, would discourage the risky behaviors and benefit society as a whole.

Another group thinks society, not smokers, should pay for tobacco-related illness. They point out that nicotine is addictive, and addiction takes away choice, particularly in those who became addicted as children or teens. Some addiction may be genetic. Addicted people may be manipulated by advertising or peer pressure. This group feels that penalizing smokers blames the victims while ignoring the causes of their behavior. They feel the harm to smokers from such penalties would be greater than the benefit to society.

HOW TO QUIT

There are many ways to quit smoking, and different plans work for different people. The important thing is to choose a plan and stick to it. Five approaches to quitting the nicotine habit are: cold turkey (quitting with no help); behavioral therapy; nicotine replacement therapy; medication; and combining one or more treatments. The success of these methods varies, but none will

Many organizations provide extensive resources and information for people who are considering quitting smoking.

be successful unless the smoker is ready to quit. If the person fears the withdrawal process or simply enjoys smoking too much to quit, any method will fail.

About 90 percent of those who want to quit smoking try the cold turkey approach first. But only four to seven percent are successful.[5] The Quit Smoking Community suggests the following guidelines for using this approach. First, become educated about nicotine addiction and its effects. Second, set a timeline and be prepared for withdrawal symptoms. Manage cravings by methods such as drinking water, finding distractions, or breathing deeply. Third, do not relapse by smoking just one cigarette. This puts nicotine back into the body, starting the withdrawal process all over again. Finally, changing one's daily routine, seeking support from friends and family, and celebrating milestones with small rewards makes success more likely.

SIDE EFFECTS OF QUITTING SMOKING

Smoking is addictive and quitting is difficult. It causes both physical and psychological withdrawal symptoms. Usually, the first 72 hours are the worst. Symptoms include depression or boredom. People trying to quit might become anxious, irritable, or even angry. They might have headaches or tremors, or feel too hot or cold. They might have indigestion, bleeding gums, or trouble sleeping. They will probably feel generally tired and uncomfortable. To make it through these symptoms, it helps to create new daily rituals to replace smoking, or do something special and fun to divert one's attention from smoking.

In behavioral therapy, the smoker works with a counselor to figure out triggers, factors that make the person crave a cigarette. Together, they develop a plan for quitting. In cognitive behavioral therapy (CBT), people learn to change their thought processes and learn positive behaviors to replace the negative behavior of smoking. CBT is usually most effective when combined with other methods, such as medication or nicotine replacement therapy.

Medications require a doctor's prescription. They decrease cravings and control withdrawal symptoms. Two medications often used are Chantix and Zyban. Nicotine replacement therapy involves replacing the nicotine in cigarettes with nicotine from another source. This might be nicotine gum, a patch, an inhaler, or lozenges. Nicotine gum, lozenges, and patches do not require a prescription, but inhalers do. Inhalers deliver nicotine as a mist into the mouth and throat. Replacement therapies contain much less nicotine than cigarettes. They cause the release of the same brain chemicals as nicotine, but in lesser amounts. This dampens withdrawal symptoms and weans the smoker off nicotine gradually. However, nicotine replacements have only been tested on adults, so doctors do not recommend them for anyone under 18.

Some forms of nicotine replacement double a smoker's chances of quitting. The method works best when two replacements are combined. It is also more successful when done

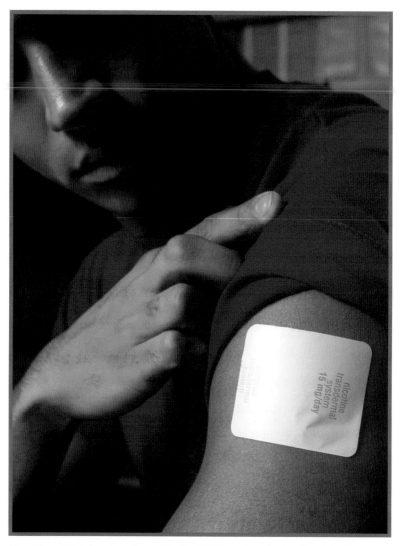

Nicotine patches, developed in the 1980s, release nicotine into the body through the skin.

alongside a complete program for quitting, plus help from a

counselor, doctor, or support group.

If an FDA plan announced in August 2017 comes to pass,

tobacco addiction may become less of a problem in the future.

FDA chief Dr. Scott Gottlieb hopes to put a legal limit on the amount of nicotine allowed in cigarettes. The Tobacco Control Act prevents the FDA from removing all nicotine from cigarettes, but it can set a maximum level in the interest of public health. This level could be too low to create or maintain addiction. The tobacco industry is expected to fight this plan, but companies would still be able to sell nicotine in other forms, including in e-cigarettes. Some members of the tobacco industry are beginning to think of a time beyond cigarettes.

They are starting to develop and sell smoke-free products. An executive at tobacco company Phillip Morris says, "We are absolutely serious—one day we want to stop selling cigarettes."[6]

A SMOKE-FREE FUTURE

In 2016, Phillip Morris International Inc. sold $26 billion in cigarettes. But the company is positioning itself for a smoke-free future. Its solution: the IQOS (pronounced I-kose), a tobacco-delivery device that includes a palm-sized charger. The user inserts a flavored tobacco packet into the IQOS and presses a button. A metal blade inside heats the tobacco to about one-third the temperature of a cigarette. The user puffs on the heated tobacco. Because the tobacco is not burned, it produces no fire, smoke, or ash, so Phillip Morris claims it is safer than cigarettes.

ESSENTIAL FACTS

EFFECTS ON THE BODY

- Tobacco affects every cell and organ of the body. Nicotine, the addictive ingredient in tobacco, is also a potent toxin. Smoking tobacco contains more than 7,000 chemicals, at least 69 of which are carcinogenic.

- Worldwide, tobacco is a risk factor for six of the eight leading causes of death, including coronary heart disease, cardiovascular disease, lower respiratory infections, COPD, tuberculosis, and cancers. Lung cancer kills about 1.2 million people around the world every year. In the United States, 80 to 90 percent of lung cancer deaths are tobacco related. Tobacco use also causes cancers of the mouth and throat, stomach, colon and rectum, liver, pancreas, and kidneys.

LAWS AND POLICIES

- Since the 1960s, when the first major studies on the health effects of tobacco were published, governments have begun to regulate tobacco use. Laws are designed to improve public health by preventing people (especially youths) from beginning tobacco use, helping tobacco users quit, and reducing the harmful effects of tobacco use. The first regulations, introduced in the 1960s, required warning labels on cigarette packages. In 2009, the United States passed the Tobacco Control Act, which restricted marketing of tobacco products to youth, required labels on smokeless tobacco products, required evidence for "modified risk" claims, and required tobacco producers to list their products' ingredients.

- Laws and regulations have also designated certain areas as being smoke free. In the 1970s, cities and states began to enact tobacco bans. As of mid-2017, about 81.6 percent of the US population was covered by laws banning smoking in workplaces, bars, restaurants, or other locations. The Campaign for Tobacco-Free Kids gives evidence that these bans reduce smoking and discourage youth from smoking.

IMPACT ON SOCIETY

- Smoking and other tobacco use impacts society both economically and socially. The United States spends $170 billion per year on medical care for adults with tobacco-related illnesses. Businesses lose another $156 billion per year due to medical costs for their employees, lost work time, and other tobacco-related costs. Overall, smoking rates are decreasing, but many young people are switching from regular cigarettes to e-cigarettes, which are also addictive and cause health problems.

- Another societal factor is the cost of secondhand smoke—how smoking affects nonsmokers. Nonsmokers who breathe in secondhand smoke receive the same toxins and are subject to the same diseases as smokers. Every year, 3,000 nonsmokers die from lung cancer due to secondhand smoke, and another 46,000 die from heart disease. Children are especially vulnerable to secondhand smoke. As evidence about the health effects of smoking increased, nonsmokers became more vocal about the dangers of secondhand smoke and their right to breathe clean, smoke-free air.

QUOTE

"The cigarette is the only consumer product that kills when used as directed— half of its long-term users, in fact."

—Dr. Scott Gottlieb, FDA Chief

ADDICTION
A compulsive need for a habit-forming substance, such as nicotine or alcohol.

ATHEROSCLEROSIS
The buildup of plaque on arterial walls, resulting in the narrowing of the arteries and the slowing or sometimes blocking of blood flow.

CANCER
Uncontrolled mitosis, or cell division, resulting in the formation of malignant tumors.

CARCINOGENIC
Cancer causing.

CARDIOVASCULAR
Relating to the heart or blood vessels.

CHRONIC
Continuing for a long time.

EMPHYSEMA
A progressive, incurable lung condition in which the alveoli (air sacs) are damaged or ruptured, resulting in decreased lung capacity and shortness of breath.

MITOSIS

Cell division; the normal process by which cells reproduce themselves, forming two identical daughter cells.

MUTAGENIC

Able to change the genetic material (DNA) of cells, causing them to increase the rate at which they mutate, or change.

PLACENTA

An organ that connects a developing fetus to a mother, providing nutrients and carrying away waste.

SMOKELESS TOBACCO

Forms of tobacco that are taken into the body by chewing or holding them in the mouth, rather than by burning the tobacco.

STROKE

A blockage of an artery supplying the brain or some part of it.

SELECTED BIBLIOGRAPHY

"Health Risks of Smoking Tobacco." *American Cancer Society*. American Cancer Society, 2015. Web. 30 Oct. 2017.

"Nicotine Dependence." *Mayo Clinic*. Mayo Clinic, 2017. Web. 30 Oct. 2017.

"Smoking and Tobacco Use." *CDC*. CDC, 2017. Web. 30 Oct. 2017.

FURTHER READINGS

Espejo, Roman. *Tobacco and Smoking*. Farmington Hills, MI: Greenhaven, 2015. Print.

Snyder, Gail. *Teens and Smoking*. San Diego, CA: ReferencePoint Press, 2016. Print.

Streissguth, Tom. *Inside the Tobacco Industry*. Minneapolis, MN: Abdo, 2017. Print.

ONLINE RESOURCES

Booklinks
NONFICTION NETWORK
FREE! ONLINE NONFICTION RESOURCES

To learn more about tobacco, visit **abdobooklinks.com**. These links are routinely monitored and updated to provide the most current information available.

MORE INFORMATION

For more information on this subject, contact or visit the following organizations:

CAMPAIGN FOR TOBACCO-FREE KIDS

1400 I Street NW, Suite 1200
Washington, DC 20005
202-296-5469
tobaccofreekids.org/who_we_are

Founded in 1996, this organization advocates at national, state, and local levels to reduce tobacco use. It promotes government policies to control tobacco use, exposes tobacco industry attempts to market to children and mislead the public, and promotes youth leadership and activism.

OFFICE ON SMOKING AND HEALTH,
CENTERS FOR DISEASE CONTROL AND PREVENTION

1600 Clifton Road
Atlanta, GA 30329
800-CDC-INFO (800-232-4636)
cdc.gov/tobacco/about/osh/index.htm

This government website has a great deal of information on the health effects of tobacco, the prevalence of tobacco use, and how to quit smoking.

CHAPTER 1. TOBACCO OR NO TOBACCO?

1. Patti Neighmond. "One Teen's Struggle to Quit Smoking." *NPR*. NPR News, 6 Nov. 2008. Web. 10 Jan. 2018.

2. Carrie McDermott. "Tobacco 21 Initiative Spanning Country." *Daily News*. Wahpeton Daily News, 1 Aug. 2017. Web. 10 Jan. 2018.

3. Gia Miller. "Teens, Pre-Teens Support Increasing Smoking Age to 21." *UPI*. UPI, 19 June 2017. Web. 10 Jan. 2018.

4. McDermott, "Tobacco 21 Initiative Spanning Country."

5. McDermott, "Tobacco 21 Initiative Spanning Country."

6. Miller, "Teens, Pre-Teens Support Increasing Smoking Age to 21."

7. McDermott, "Tobacco 21 Initiative Spanning Country."

8. "World No Tobacco Day 2017." *UN*. UN, 30 May 2017. Web. 10 Jan. 2018.

9. "Tobacco Control Can Save Billions of Dollars and Millions of Lives." *WHO*. WHO, 10 Jan. 2017. Web. 10 Jan. 2018.

10. "Tobacco Industry Blocking Anti-Smoking Moves: WHO." *Thomson Reuters*. Thomson Reuters, 20 July 2017. Web. 10 Jan. 2018.

11. "The Constitution of Smokers Association." *Smokers Association*. Smokers Association, 24 May 2008. Web. 10 Jan. 2018.

12. "Trends in Tobacco Industry Marketing." *Campaign for Tobacco-Free Kids*. Campaign for Tobacco-Free Kids, n.d. Web. 10 Jan. 2018.

13. "Trends in Tobacco Industry Marketing."

14. Samantha K. Graff. "There Is No Constitutional Right to Smoke: 2008." *Tobacco Control Legal Consortium*. Public Health Law Center, Mar. 2008. Web. 10 Jan. 2018.

15. Thomas Greenwood. "The Right to Smoke vs. the Right to Breathe." *New York Times*. New York Times, 8 May 1988. Web. 10 Jan. 2018.

16. "Current Cigarette Smoking among Adults in the United States." *CDC*. CDC, 1 Dec. 2016. Web. 10 Jan. 2018.

17. Maggie Fox. "US Teens Dump Tobacco, E-Cigarettes." *NBC News*. NBC, 16 June 2017. Web. 10 Jan. 2018.

18. Fox, "US Teens Dump Tobacco, E-Cigarettes."

CHAPTER 2. WHAT IS TOBACCO?

1. "Tobacco Industry." *Statista*. Statista, 31 Aug. 2017. Web. 10 Jan. 2018.

2. "How Cigarettes Are Made and How You Can Make a Plan to Quit." *FDA*. FDA, 19 Dec. 2017. Web. 10 Jan. 2018.

3. "What's in a Cigarette?" *American Lung Association*. American Lung Association, 2018. Web. 10 Jan. 2018.

4. Terry Martin. "Harmful Chemicals in Cigarettes." *Verywell*. Verywell, 10 Jan. 2017. Web. 10 Jan. 2018.

5. Gregory R. Lande. "Nicotine Addiction." *Medscape*. Medscape, 10 Aug. 2017. Web. 10 Jan. 2018.

6. "Nicotine Addiction and Your Health." *BeTobaccoFree.gov*. HHS, n.d. Web. 10 Jan. 2018.

7. "Types of Tobacco Products." *Department of Public Health*. State of Connecticut, n.d. Web. 10 Jan. 2018.

8. Helen Minciotti. "Popularity of Smokeless Tobacco on the Rise." *Daily Herald*. Daily Herald, 29 Aug. 2011. Web. 10 Jan. 2018.

CHAPTER 3. TOBACCO IN AMERICA

1. "History of the Surgeon General's Reports on Smoking and Health." *CDC*. CDC, 6 July 2009. Web. 10 Jan. 2018.

2. Denise Grady. "Smoking's Toll on Health Is Even Worse Than Previously Thought, a Study Finds." *New York Times*. New York Times, 11 Feb. 2015. Web. 10 Jan. 2018.

3. "Youth and Tobacco Use." *CDC*. CDC, 20 June 2017. Web. 10 Jan. 2018.

4. "Teens and E-Cigarettes." *National Institute on Drug Use*. NIH, Feb. 2016. Web. 10 Jan. 2018.

5. Grady, "Smoking's Toll on Health."

6. Grady, "Smoking's Toll on Health."

7. "Tips from Former Smokers." *CDC*. CDC, 27 July 2017. Web. 10 Jan. 2018.

8. "A Brief History of Smoking." *Cancer Council Australia*. Cancer Council Australia, 2015. Web. 10 Jan. 2018.

CHAPTER 4. TOBACCO AND CANCER

1. "Tobacco as a Cause of Lung Cancer." *Lung Cancer Answers*. Lung Cancer Answers, n.d. Web. 5 Sept. 2017.

2. L. Crinò, et al. "Early State and Locally Advanced (Non-Metastatic) Non-Small-Cell Lung Cancer." *Annals of Oncology*, vol. 21, issue supplement 5, 2010, pp. 105–133.

3. "Key Statistics for Lung Cancer." *American Cancer Society*. American Cancer Society, 5 Jan. 2017. Web. 10 Jan. 2018.

4. "Cancer and Tobacco Use." *CDC*. CDC, 10 Nov. 2016. Web. 10 Jan. 2018.

5. "Cancer and Tobacco Use."

6. "Cancer and Tobacco Use."

7. "Tobacco as a Cause of Lung Cancer."

8. "Cancer Survival Rate: What It Means for Your Prognosis." *Mayo Clinic*. Mayo Clinic, 15 Apr. 2014. Web. 10 Jan. 2018.

9. "Tobacco and Cancer: What Are the Survival Rates?" *Truth Initiative*. Truth Initiative, 22 May 2017. Web. 10 Jan. 2018.

10. "Tobacco as a Cause of Lung Cancer."

CHAPTER 5. TOBACCO AND RESPIRATORY DISEASE

1. "Face to Face with COPD." *WHO*. WHO, 2017. Web. 10 Jan. 2018.

2. "Deaths and Mortality." *National Center for Health Statistics*. CDC, 3 May 2017. Web. 10 Jan. 2018.

CHAPTER 6. TOBACCO AND CIRCULATORY DISEASE

1. Liz Szabo. "Smoking Bans Cut Number of Heart Attacks, Strokes." *USA Today*. USA Today, 29 Oct. 2012. Web. 10 Jan. 2018.

2. "Smoking and Cardiovascular Disease." *Johns Hopkins Medicine*. Johns Hopkins, n.d. Web. 10 Jan. 2018.

3. "Effects of Smoking Pipes and Cigars." *WebMD*. WebMD, 10 Oct. 2016. Web. 10 Jan. 2018.

4. Chris Woolston. "The Risks of Cigars." *HealthDay*. HealthDay, 20 Jan. 2017. Web. 10 Jan. 2018.

5. "Risk Factors." *World Heart Federation*. World Heart Federation, n.d. Web. 10 Jan. 2018.

6. "Women and Smoking." *CDC*. CDC, 2014. Web. 10 Jan. 2018.

CHAPTER 7. TOBACCO AND OTHER HEALTH PROBLEMS

1. "Tobacco-Related Mortality." *CDC*. CDC, 1 Dec. 2016. Web. 10 Jan. 2018.

2. Dominic Hughes. "Smoking and Health 50 Years on from Landmark Report." *BBC News*. BBC, 6 Mar. 2012. Web. 10 Jan. 2018.

3. Allan Hackshaw, Charles Rodeck, and Sadie Boniface. "Maternal Smoking in Pregnancy and Birth Defects." *Human Reproduction Update* 17.5 (2011): 589–604.

4. "Smoking and Periodontitis." *DentistryIQ*. DentistryIQ, 1 Feb. 2004. Web. 10 Jan. 2018.

CHAPTER 8. SOCIAL AND LEGAL IMPLICATIONS

1. "Tobacco Industry Blocking Anti-Smoking Moves: WHO."

2. "Smoking and Tobacco Use." *Fast Facts*. CDC, 2017. Web. 10 Jan. 2018.

3. "Smoking and Tobacco Use."

4. Mary Elizabeth Dallas. "Smokers Cost Employers More Than Nonsmokers." *WebMD*. WebMD, 2013. Web. 10 Jan. 2018.

5. John R. Hall, Jr. "The Smoking-Material Fire Problem." *National Fire Protection Association*. NFPA, July 2013. Web. 10 Jan. 2018.

6. Elizabeth Fernandez. "Health Care Costs Drop Quickly after Smokers Quit." *Center for Tobacco Control Research and Education*. USCF, 10 May 2016. Web. 10 Jan. 2018.

7. Sophie Egan. "The Cost of a Smoker: $5,816." *New York Times*. New York Times, 7 Aug. 2013. Web. 10 Jan. 2018.

8. "Smoking and Tobacco Use."

9. "Secondhand Smoke Facts." *CDC*. CDC, 21 Feb. 2017. Web. 10 Jan. 2018.

10. "Secondhand Smoke and Cancer." *National Institutes of Health*. NIH, 12 Jan. 2011. Web. 10 Jan. 2018.

11. Dallas. "Smokers Cost Employers More Than Nonsmokers."

12. Deborah M. Scharf and William Shadel. "Graphic Warning Labels on Cigarettes Are Scary, But Do They Work?" *Rand Corporation*. Rand Corporation, 30 Sept. 2014. Web. 10 Jan. 2018.

13. "The Facts on the FDA's New Tobacco Rule." *FDA*. FDA, 9 Nov. 2017. Web. 10 Jan. 2018.

14. Katharine Q. Seelye. "Firestorm Erupts in Anti-Smoking Massachusetts Town." *New York Times*. New York Times, 17 Nov. 2014. Web. 10 Jan. 2018.

15. Seelye. "Firestorm Erupts in Anti-Smoking Massachusetts Town."

16. "Smokefree Lists, Maps, and Data." *American Nonsmokers' Rights Foundation*. ANRF, 2 Jan. 2018. Web. 31 Jan. 2018.

CHAPTER 9. QUITTING SMOKING

1. John R. Polito. "Nineteen-Year-Old Sean Marsee's Cancer Message." *WhyQuit*. WhyQuit, 5 Jan. 2014. Web. 10 Jan. 2018.

2. Robert N. Proctor. "Taking the Addiction Out of Smoking." *New York Times*. New York Times, 2 Aug. 2017. Web. 10 Jan. 2018.

3. "Preventing Tobacco Use among Youth and Young Adults." *Surgeon General*. CDC, 2012. Web. 10 Jan. 2018.

4. "The Path to Tobacco Addiction Starts at Very Young Ages." *Campaign for Tobacco-Free Kids*. Campaign for Tobacco-Free Kids, n.d. Web. 10 Jan. 2018.

5. "How to Quit Smoking." *WebMD*. WebMD, 2016. Web. 10 Jan. 2018.

6. Proctor. "Taking the Addiction Out of Smoking."

INDEX

ABOUT THE AUTHOR

Carol Hand has a PhD in zoology. She has taught college biology (including courses on human anatomy and physiology and on drugs), written biology assessments for national assessment companies, written middle and high school science curricula for a national company, and authored more than 40 young-adult science books, including several on health topics. Currently she works as a freelance science writer.